My sheep listen
to my voice; I know them,
and they follow me. I give them
eternal life, and they
will never perish.

JOHN 10:27-28

HEARING HIS VOICE

HEARING

His

VOICE

90 DEVOTIONS TO DEEPEN
YOUR CONNECTION
WITH GOD

CHRIS TIEGREEN

TYNDALE
MOMENTUM®

The Tyndale nonfiction imprint

Visit Tyndale online at tyndale.com.

Visit Tyndale Momentum online at tyndalemomentum.com.

TYNDALE, Tyndale's quill logo, *Tyndale Momentum*, and the Tyndale Momentum logo are registered trademarks of Tyndale House Publishers. Tyndale Momentum is the nonfiction imprint of Tyndale House Publishers, Carol Stream, Illinois.

Hearing His Voice: 90 Devotions to Deepen Your Connection with God

Devotional content adapted from *The One Year Hearing His Voice Devotional* published by Tyndale House Publishers in 2014 under ISBN 978-1-4964-2093-0.

Designed by Ron C. Kaufmann

Published in association with the literary agency of Mark Sweeney and Associates.

For information about special discounts for bulk purchases, please contact Tyndale House Publishers at csresponse@tyndale.com, or call 1-800-323-9400.

ISBN 978-1-4964-4696-1

Printed in China

26   25   24   23   22   21   20
7   6   5   4   3   2   1

INTRODUCTION

I once heard a very prominent pastor scoff at Christians who "think they can actually hear God directly." But isn't it true that the entire Christian faith is based on the belief that God wants a personal relationship with His people? If so, it seems natural to ask ourselves what kind of relationship He wants. One without conversation? Surely not. That would hardly be a relationship. No, God speaks, and His people listen. That's what following Him is all about.

Though many in the Western church insist that God doesn't speak directly to us today—because our hearing is too subjective, or He has already said everything He has to say in the Bible—Christians in less rigidly analytical and skeptical cultures are hearing God daily and doing mighty works in the power of His Spirit, simply by following what they hear. Yes, we can find examples of abuses and stories of people who misheard God, but there are far more testimonies of people who have heard God clearly and have borne much fruit from what they have heard.

Anyone can learn to recognize God's voice. And God doesn't mind the skeptics. He simply speaks to people who will listen and believe.

What does God say to us? How does He say it? How can we know when we've heard Him? What can we do to hear Him better? We could spend the rest of our lives learning how to recognize God's voice, but if we seek Him, we can be confident that He will make Himself available to us. If we listen, He will speak. And if we believe what we have heard, He will show us even more. God always seeks to take us deeper into His will and draw us closer to Himself.

This book includes ninety devotional readings that cover many issues related to hearing God. One of every nine devotions is written as a first-person perspective from the heart of God—things I have sensed Him saying and that I believe He wants to share with those who will listen. Sometimes people are uncomfortable with this approach, but it fits well with New Testament practice (see 1 Corinthians 14:1 and 1 Peter 4:11). God is not bothered by our efforts to express His thoughts.

Each devotion ends with a brief prayer. Some people—like me, sometimes—tend to skip over guided prayers in books, but I encourage you not to do that here. Some of the prayers may seem simple or superfluous, but there is a point to them. When we ask from God, we receive. He responds when we express our desires to Him. If your desire is to hear God's voice, then asking to hear Him better, no matter how basic the request, is an invaluable practice. If some of the prayers seem repetitive, that's okay. We're told in Scripture to keep asking, to persist until God answers. Over the course of ninety days, He will answer—often in surprising ways.

Listening to God is a process, a journey, and an adventure. It may take time, but it's worth the effort. He promises that those who seek Him will be rewarded with His presence and His voice. The words of the living God are powerful and life-changing. May He bless your desire to hear Him.

In the beginning the Word already existed.

The Word was with God, and the Word was God.

JOHN 1:1

From the first pages of Scripture, God speaks. Every time He utters a word, things happen. He says, "Let there be light," and light comes into being—and He keeps talking until our entire universe is filled with order and life. He calls out a people from among the nations and reveals His purposes through them. He chooses prophets to deliver His messages when those people are in danger and need to return to Him. And when He sends His own Son to live among us, the Son is called "the Word." Clearly, we do not serve a silent God.

Many people can't say with any certainty that God still speaks today, much less to them personally. They can accept His written Word as His voice—generalized for all who read it, of course—but for personal conversations and direction, they strive and strain to hear. Our theology tells us that God is quite vocal, even if our experience tells us He isn't. The result of this paradox is a lot of theory, little practice, and a considerable amount of frustration.

Step one in hearing God is acknowledging that He still speaks. We must be convinced of that in order to press through the frustrations on the way to hearing Him. Low expectations will undermine our efforts. If we know He's the Word who always has something to say, we won't give up easily in our attempts to hear Him. Most of all, we'll *believe*—a prerequisite to receiving anything from God. Faith opens our ears.

Believe not only that God still speaks, but that He's speaking *to you*. He calls you into a relationship, and relationships are based on communication. Conversations with God are normal—you were designed for them. Believe and listen—and know that you will hear.

Living Word, I invite You to speak to me. I know You have been; please open my ears to hear. I want to learn the sound of Your voice and know Your thoughts. In faith, I'm listening.

DAY 2

*A*cquaintances share pleasantries. Close friends share personal information. We would be surprised and somewhat offended if an acquaintance tried to pry personal information out of us before getting to know us and establishing a relationship of trust. Yet this is what many of us do with God; we come with frequent prayer requests and ask Him to speak about things concerning our own small spheres of interest. Few of us take time to ask Him what's on His heart, to be good listeners, and to show real interest in the aspects of His will that don't pertain to us. We can assume God doesn't *need* to be surrounded with good listeners, as if He would want to get something off His chest or seek counsel. But God created us for relationship—deep, personal interaction—and though He doesn't need our counsel, He seeks our interest. He wants to connect with those who share His heart.

There's a reason John was leaning back against Jesus at the Last Supper and was thus privy to inside information about the betrayer. John was "the disciple whom Jesus loved" (John 13:23, NIV), one of the men who had developed a real friendship with the Messiah. This was no mere acquaintance probing Jesus for personal secrets. This was a follower who was truly interested in the heart of his friend and who interacted with Him on multiple levels—not just when he needed something, but at any time and for any reason. John did not relate to Jesus as a servant under orders. He related as a friend with quite a few interests in common. And that put him in a position to hear.

That's how it is with us, too. When we relate to Jesus as a friend, truly interested in what's on His heart, He shares His heart with us. And we connect at a very personal level.

> *Jesus, what's on Your heart today? I really want to know.*
> *Please share it with me.*

It is God's privilege to conceal things and the king's

privilege to discover them.

PROVERBS 25:2

God has a strange tendency to hide from those who are seeking Him and relentlessly pursue those who are not. Perhaps He enjoys the playful give-and-take of a spiritual hide-and-seek. Or maybe He simply insists on being found on His own terms. More likely, He is like a suitor who seeks out the object of His affection but won't overplay the intensity of His desire. There must be a genuine response from His beloved, not a forced one. Even so, He conceals Himself—His voice, His specific will, His reasons—in ways that are sometimes frustratingly obscure for us. He gives us a taste of His goodness, opens our ears to hear, and then steps back. He pursues us and then withdraws, provoking an intensity in our desire that drives us deeper into His heart. He conceals things and waits for us to seek them out.

The proverb above specifically mentions kings, but it reveals God's nature as it applies to all of us. He doesn't normally thunder His voice from the heavens; He hides it in secret places and waits to see who is hungry for it. Who will persist in the search to hear Him? Who really wants to feel His heartbeat and understand His will? Who desires a relationship, rather than a set of principles to live by? These are questions that are answered only in the searching. Those who are content with religious practices will give up early in the quest. Those who can be satisfied only with God will persist until they really encounter Him. That's the way it works.

God conceals deep secrets and then subtly provokes us to discover them. Will we continue in that search without losing heart? At times, that's the very issue for the one who wants to hear Him speak. And the response must always drive us closer.

Lord, I'll never give up my desire for more of You—
more closeness, better hearing, a deeper connection.
Draw me closer and show me the secrets of Your heart.

We are confident that he hears us whenever we ask for anything that pleases

him. And since we know he hears us when we make our requests, we also

know that he will give us what we ask for.

I JOHN 5:14-15

*F*or most of us, the normal pattern of prayer is to ask God to
accomplish certain things and then wait to see what He does
with our requests. There's nothing wrong with that approach;
any kind of conversation with God qualifies as prayer. But those
petitions are almost like shooting an arrow in the dark and hoping it hits the bull's-eye. Is it His will, or isn't it? We'll have to see
when—and if—the results come in.

According to biblical promises, God means for our prayers
to be more confident than that. His Word tells us that a prayer
of faith often is answered when a tentative prayer would not be.
But for us to pray in faith, we must know up front whether our
petitions are consistent with God's will. When we pray and only
hope He will answer if the request happens to fit within His will,
it's hard to pray in faith. We trust God, of course, but we don't
have much confidence that our prayer will be answered. In order
to have specific faith for what we ask, we need to know that
what we ask fits God's purposes.

This is one of the areas in which it is crucial for us to hear God's voice. We know His general purposes through His Word—clearly, we can be confident about some requests that further His Kingdom. But the personal requests about direction, provision, healing, and more—not to mention the deep longings of our hearts—are always tentative unless we've heard from Him. He invites us to ask what His will is—and then, when we've heard, to pray that His will be done. Confidently.

Father, if you tell me my prayer is consistent with Your will, I will maintain unwavering faith until the answer shows up. Help me pray Your desires and mine with confidence.

Whenever the cloud lifted from the Tabernacle, the people of Israel would

set out on their journey, following it. But if the cloud did not rise, they

remained where they were until it lifted.

EXODUS 40:36-37

We have decisions to make, so we ask for guidance. We wait for it. We remind God of His promises to give wisdom to those who seek it. And when He lingers . . . well, very often we don't let Him linger. We assume that if He hasn't spoken quickly, He must be leaving us to our own discernment to make the best decision we can. We go ahead and move forward, not because we've heard His voice but because moving forward seems to be the only option. We use our best judgment and trust that it fits with His will.

Sometimes God wants us to move forward in the wisdom and discernment we already have, but our decision-making process should never be reduced to that alone. We are in such a rush to make decisions that we act as if meeting a deadline is more important than hearing specific direction from God. When He lingers, He is waiting to see if we will fill the vacuum by seeking Him or by using our own logic and sense of urgency. Far too often, we fill the gaps with our own assumptions. We make decisions before we've heard God's directions.

When the Israelites were following God in the wilderness, they waited until the cloud rose and led them. If the cloud didn't rise, the people didn't either. They stayed, sometimes long beyond their own comfort level, until God led them. That isn't easy to do, but it's an essential exercise in faith and listening. In most significant decisions, God wants us to ask and wait. And wait some more. And wait even more—until we've heard. No time is wasted in this process; when we follow the "cloud" of direction, God gives us a direct path into His will.

Lord, You direct my paths, sometimes much more methodically than I want. Give me a patient spirit; help me not rush to judgment; undo my assumptions. And when I've heard from You, I'll follow with confidence.

[Jesus said,] "I am leaving you with a gift—peace of mind

and heart. And the peace I give is a gift the world cannot give.

So don't be troubled or afraid."

JOHN 14:27

Christians give a lot of attention to hearing what God says, but much less to recognizing His tone of voice. But the two are linked, and we will scarcely be able to understand what the Lord says if we aren't listening to how He says it. In human relationships, the same words can mean entirely different things if they are spoken in anger rather than with a sense of humor, or with disdain rather than gentle encouragement. As one social commentator suggested, the medium is the message. *How* something is said is often more significant than the words themselves.

So when we hear God's voice, we need to know the tone of voice it carries. In other words, we need to be able to "see" the expression on His face. He gives us plenty of clues for that throughout His Word, and this verse is one of them. Jesus said He was leaving His followers with peace of mind and heart. He didn't want them to be troubled or afraid. We can reasonably conclude, then, that His voice is not going to produce turmoil or anxiety in us. It isn't going to be caustic or critical. He isn't an alarmist who spins us into a panic when something goes wrong. He will calm our fears and soothe our turbulent spirits. His words will sound like they come from the mouth of the Mighty Savior who rejoices over us with singing and quiets us with His love (Zephaniah 3:17).

Refuse to listen to the alarmists of our day who urge God's people to panic over elections, antichrists, or social decay. If there are trials, God will be with us in them. If there are battles, they will end in victory. He will not spare us from trouble, but He will certainly help us overcome it. And He will speak peace to our hearts.

Jesus, I need Your peace. I cast aside all false voices—words of panic, turmoil, and condemnation. I love the sound of Your true voice.

DAY 7

Don't be afraid; just believe.

MARK 5:36, NIV

*I*t seemed like the death of a dream. I had been filled with hope about a certain situation, trusting God to work it out according to His purpose and my desire. But a shift in circumstances turned the situation in the opposite, and seemingly tragic, direction. How could this possibly be God's will? Should I give up hope? Was I still supposed to believe the things I thought God had said, even though they now seemed impossible?

The next day, I went to see a movie with my family. I was hurting inside, begging God to give me direction. When a character in the movie lost something that was precious to him, I heard in my spirit, *Watch what happens now; this is for you.* And when the lost item was soon miraculously restored, I took heart. Later, the same character faced an impossible situation, and once again, my spirit heard the words, *This is for you.* In the next few seconds, that character was told by another, "Only believe." I knew God was speaking.

Even though movies—or books or TV shows or any other form of entertainment—aren't inspired like Scripture is, they can contain biblical themes or even seemingly random words that

God applies to specific situations. He makes words and scenes come alive in a deeply personal way to the reader or viewer who needs to hear Him. And when we are questioning faith we once held, whether it's in a promise that God gave or a truth of His Kingdom, He encourages us to hang on. In our weakest moments, when doubts seem to overwhelm us or circumstances seem to challenge our trust in Him, He whispers, "Don't be afraid; just believe." If the dream is given by Him, He will do everything necessary to keep it alive in our hearts—including speaking through the stories in our lives.

Lord, You are a God of stories. You write stories with the lives of Your people, You tell them to teach us deep truths, and You speak to us through them when we listen carefully. Fill my life with stories that impart Your words.

When you ask, you must believe and not doubt, because the one who doubts is

like a wave of the sea, blown and tossed by the wind.

JAMES 1:6, NIV

Some people ask for God's wisdom without any assurance that they might receive it. The result? They probably won't. That's because any genuine prayer must be accompanied by faith. Otherwise, we'll second-guess the answer until it has hardly any power left.

This pattern is the unfortunate testimony of many. We ask; we hear; then we only think we heard; then we're pretty sure it was just our own conscience/thoughts/desires; then we're more confused on the matter than ever. And while it's always important to be discerning, it's never desirable to be overly analytical. Our minds and hearts can talk our spirits out of just about anything. The result is that we may hear God often but feel as if we rarely hear from Him. We're blown and tossed by the winds and waves of doubt.

God is much more intentional about communicating with us than that, and much more willing to be heard than we think He is. He speaks through the deep fountain of His Spirit whom He has placed within us, through the fellowship of believers, through signs and messages and desires, and through many other means. And of course, He speaks above all through the counsel of His Word. What more do we want? A voice that thunders from heaven? He has been known to do that, too, though rarely. He prefers to converse with us in a deeply relational way, and surely laments that while we have an enormous capacity for having a relationship with Him, we constantly question that relationship. He urges us to come, to ask, and to *believe*.

When we ask to hear His voice, we must believe and not doubt. That's His instruction to us, not our own imaginings. His Word never urges us to overanalyze; it practically pleads with us to believe. Those who ask with assurance are blessed with hearing ears.

Lord, I've asked to hear Your voice; now I'm choosing to believe. I'll trust that You will keep me from error, and I'll accept what I believe You're saying. Guide me into truth.

DAY 9

[The Lord said,] "Oh, that my people would listen to me! Oh,

that Israel would follow me, walking in my paths!"

PSALM 81:13

From the Heart of God

"Many people cry out to hear My voice, but they aren't really listeners. I speak, and they dismiss My words as their own imagination, coincidence, or subjective experience. Some even dismiss the Bible as not being My voice to them because it didn't apply specifically to them when I first spoke those words, or they don't think that context is relevant to their lives. They place higher standards on themselves than they do on My prophets, who were bold enough to act on what they thought they heard. Skeptical hearers can talk themselves out of virtually anything I say, even though they begged Me to speak in the first place. They want to hear, but they don't want to listen.

"Most people don't realize that while they are crying out to hear My voice, I am calling out for them to listen. I have no shortage of passive hearers in My Kingdom, but I'm looking for active listeners.

I want you, like stewards who refuse to bury their talents, to take some risks. If you think you probably heard Me, don't play it safe. Assume that you did. If you pursue My voice and aren't certain you heard, the way of faith is to believe I answered your request rather than believe I didn't. I want you to trust My ability to communicate more than you trust your ability to be deceived. Listen and step out on what you've heard.

"Don't be afraid. I don't punish those who dare to have faith. If you fall, I will pick you up and put you back on the right path. If you make a mistake, I won't condemn you. My grace is more than generous for those who follow Me boldly and passionately, even at the risk of being wrong. Don't just hear with your ears. Listen with your heart."

Lord, I know You value discernment, but You value trust even more. You urge me to walk by faith, not by sight. I commit to listen intently; fill me with holy boldness to act on what I hear.

Whether you turn to the right or to the left, your ears

will hear a voice behind you, saying, "This is the way; walk in it."

ISAIAH 30:21, NIV

We long to hear God's voice. We come to a fork in the road, a moment of crisis, a point of decision that requires us to take a step in one direction or another because standing still is no longer an option. We tell God that if He just lets us know one way or another—this way or that way, heads or tails—we'll do it. Yet we're still not sure. Right or left? We just don't know.

What's the problem? Maybe the Spirit within us has already let us know, but our heads keep rationalizing the possibilities. Maybe we only *think* we're willing to do what God says, but really we're approaching His voice as good advice to consider, rather than a command to follow. Or—and this is often the case—we're merely seeking *information*, while God is calling us into deeper *relationship*. The promise of His voice isn't simply for the purpose of communication; it's for communion.

That's the mistake many of us make in our approach to hearing God. We want information, and He wants a relationship. Our approach reduces our hearing to in-and-out transactions—we come, we hear, and we leave with more knowledge than we had before. But God's desire—and the reason for His delays and silences—is to draw us closer and deeper. He withholds Himself enough to keep us seeking *Him*, as opposed to seeking His words alone. It takes more effort that way, but that's the nature of relationships. In order to grow close, we must invest time, energy, and interest. And God will withhold a right-or-left answer if it provokes us to make that investment. Seek Him above all else— and His voice will eventually become clearer.

Lord, forgive me for seeking You as a giver of information rather than seeking You as a person. Draw me close, not just so I can hear Your words, but so I can hear Your heart.

All Scripture is inspired by God and is useful to teach us what is true and to

make us realize what is wrong in our lives. It corrects us when we are wrong

and teaches us to do what is right.

2 TIMOTHY 3:16

We serve a very vocal God. The world cannot contain all the words He has spoken, but we do have a record of many of them. The Bible is the written account of His words, the only authoritative source of doctrine and expression of His overall will. In it, God tells us what He is like, what His purposes are, and how we can relate to Him. He has uttered many words that weren't written in Scripture—references to prophets who spoke for Him but never wrote anything are enough to convince us of that—but what is written is reliable. In our search for His voice, the Bible is our primary source.

Still, we must learn how to *interpret* God's Word. At times, He is quoted directly. At other times, writers describe Him or tell stories about encounters people had with Him. The Bible is always true in reporting what people said or believed, but not everything they said or believed is true. For example, Job's friends had a lot to say about God and His ways, and the book of Job records their arguments accurately. Some of what they said was true, but much of it wasn't or was wrongly applied. The reader is left to discern when the person being quoted is reliable and when he or she isn't. It isn't always clear. We must ask the Holy Spirit to help us with the interpretation.

That means that even when we're reading the inspired Word of God, we still must listen for God's voice. Many are attracted to the "objectivity" of reading the written Word, but centuries of differing opinions and misguided interpretations should be enough to convince us that our objectivity isn't very objective. We need God's help to hear His voice in His Word. When we read, we must open our ears to hear.

Lord, give me understanding. Enliven Your Word and let it sink deeply into my heart.

In these final days, he has spoken to us through his Son.

HEBREWS 1:2

The writer of Hebrews talks a lot about God's voice. The fathers and prophets of long ago are not depicted as crafting theology, but as hearing God—and in a way that is relevant to all times. And it is clear throughout the letter of Hebrews that all other encounters with God point to one ultimate expression of His voice: Jesus. The Son is the perfect picture of what the Father is saying.

We need an anchor for interpreting God's voice, a lens through which we choose to see all else. That anchor, that lens, must be Jesus. Hebrews calls Him "the exact representation" of God the Father (1:3, NIV), which means that if we want to know what God is like, we simply need to look at Jesus. That suggests different things to different people, of course. Some imagine a stern expression on His face as they read His words; others imagine Him smiling; and still others see that vapid look so often depicted in the movies. His words come across with radically different implications, depending on which face one sees. But we know how Jesus responded to people who came to Him and to those who opposed Him. We know what He said about prayer, what He promised to His disciples, how He told them to love and serve, what attitudes He wants us to have, and more. The exact representation of God is described to us in the pages of the Gospels. God has spoken in that description.

He still does. The Son still speaks. He is a living Lord who dwells with us and within us, so we have no need to search for His words as if He were ancient history. But His words are in those books, they are still alive and active, and they still speak loudly. If we want to hear God, we can surely hear Him there.

> *Jesus, speak to me through the pages of Scripture. Let me see the expression of Your face and hear the tone of Your voice as I read. Make those words come alive in my heart.*

DAY 13

Those who obey God's word truly show how completely they love him. That is

how we know we are living in him. Those who say they live in God should

live their lives as Jesus did.

1 JOHN 2:5-6

*J*esus asked His followers a penetrating question: "Why do you keep calling me 'Lord, Lord!' when you don't do what I say?" (Luke 6:46). It seems obvious that calling Him *Lord* would necessitate following Him as Lord, but most of us aren't nearly so consistent. And though Jesus certainly understands our imperfections, there's a difference between falling short and not even trying. To hear God's voice without doing what He says is at best negligent and at worst hypocritical.

John had harsh words to say about this phenomenon. If someone claims to know God but doesn't heed God's words, he writes, "that person is a liar and is not living in the truth" (1 John 2:4). But if we saturate ourselves in His words—both written and spoken—and make it our zealous mission to carry them out, we demonstrate our love. This cultivates the kind of relationship in which communication flourishes. Any expression of good faith in friendship makes the friendship stronger.

And when we declare with our actions that we are serious about doing what God says, what He says becomes a lot easier to hear.

That doesn't mean God only wants to tell us what to do. Life with Him is not all about commands. Far from it, in fact. His greater desire is to share His heart with us. But we can't listen to Him selectively, as if His words were a shopping list from which to pick and choose. When we listen for God's promises and encouragement without heeding His instructions, we generally hear nothing at all. But when we accept the whole package of what His voice brings us, we get the whole package. We tend to approach Him to hear what we want to hear. He approaches us with an all-or-nothing proposition. To hear Him, we need to hear on His terms.

Lord, I want it all—everything You say. I'll take the difficult with the easy because it's all from You. Tell me Your joys, Your secrets, and Your commands.

The LORD thundered from heaven; the voice of the Most High resounded.

PSALM 18:13

*D*avid was in a terrible predicament. He had been pursued by enemies for years, surrounded and outnumbered at times, and hiding in caves and at oases at others. As he always did in seemingly hopeless situations, he cried out to God. And as Psalm 18 describes, God answered with power and a flair for the dramatic.

It's the ultimate answer to prayer: A child of God cries out, and God answers with thunder and lightning and earthquakes. The rescuer God rides in on a heavenly chariot and routs the enemy. In words reminiscent of the Exodus and the deliverance at the Red Sea, David applies God's power to his own situation, which on the surface wasn't nearly as dramatic. But in the behind-the-scenes war, it was just as significant. David survived his enemies and became king because God went to war using the power of His voice.

That's how God fights. Just one word from His mouth can turn a situation around completely. The mountains and seas and all the forces of nature are at His command. His angels respond decisively to His every word. When God speaks, things happen.

We long for such answers to prayer. When we cry out for God's voice, it isn't just so He will give us direction; it's also for Him to speak into the situations of our lives to change them. We can ask Him to issue commands and utter decrees that shape our circumstances and turn our predicaments into opportunities. We can even give audible voice to His promises and decrees, speaking His words into the predicaments of our lives. Under God's authority, all creation must respond to His voice. When we speak His words, creation must respond to us, as well. The thunder of God's voice changes the world around us.

Lord, let Your words resound for me, in me, and through me. Speak into my situation. Just one word from You changes everything, and I need change. Ride into my battles in the power of Your word.

As the deer longs for streams of water, so I long for you, O God. I thirst for God,

the living God. When can I go and stand before him?

PSALM 42:1-2

Sometimes we long to be rescued. Or healed. Or provided for. And sometimes we simply long for God. We recognize our need, even when we've been fully satisfied with the best the world has to offer. Money, possessions, status, recognition, accomplishments, and even meaningful human relationships aren't enough. Virtually everyone, no matter how successful, has asked the question, "Is this all there is?" We have deeper needs than we know how to satisfy.

So we thirst. Sometimes we can't put a finger on what we're thirsting for, but we know it's beyond our own resources. If we're spiritually minded, we realize that we're thirsting for God Himself, longing for the One our hearts were designed to connect with. And it's more than just a connection we desire. It's a deep, meaningful, lasting relationship that goes beyond superficial interaction. We need two-way communication, shared thoughts and dreams, a bond that can't be broken. We need to be known at the deepest level and embraced there.

God designed us with this thirst for a reason. It's what drives us closer to Him. Many give up the quest, thinking that if God hasn't shown Himself more fully, He can't be more fully known. But that isn't true. We hear Him by longing for Him. His voice resonates within us when we have decided He is more important to us than anything else.

Never forget that the ability to hear God is not a matter of technique; it's a matter of desire. Yes, there are ways to listen, attitudes that position us to hear, and perspectives that put His words in the right light. But before all that is the thirst. If it's strong enough, we won't stop listening, even if hearing is difficult. We will long for streams of water until we find them.

Lord, satisfy this quest. My relentless thirst is for You. Quench it with gushing streams of Your wisdom and inspiration. Let Your words fulfill my deepest desires.

DAY 16

You can identify [false prophets] by their fruit.

MATTHEW 7:16

$\mathcal{W}$e hear lots of voices. We suspect God's voice is in the mix somewhere, but we have a hard time distinguishing the others. Are we hearing our own thoughts? The deceptions of the enemy? The echoes of people who have tried to be our conscience in the past? The voices of temptation? How can we discern God's voice in the cacophony of alternate messages?

Jesus told His followers they would recognize false prophets by their fruit. The same advice applies to false voices of any kind. Clearly, if the messages we hear are enticing us to sin, we know they aren't from God. That's easy enough. But what about the seemingly morally neutral ones? What about when we are asking for direction and every option might be allowed but not necessarily advisable? What about the voices that speak to our identity or our behavior, and that may sound like Scripture, but also may be distortions of it? One key to discernment is to look at the fruit.

Consider the fruit of the Kingdom: goodness, peace, and joy in the Holy Spirit (Romans 14:17); the fruit of the Spirit: love, joy, peace, patience, kindness, goodness, faithfulness, gentleness, and self-control (Galatians 5:22-23); and the fruit of a redeemed mind: thoughts about whatever is true, honorable, right, pure, lovely, and admirable (Philippians 4:8). If the voice leads you toward spiritual fruitfulness, it's probably God speaking. If it doesn't—if it leads to fear, guilt, doubt, anxiety, exasperation, and the sorts of attitudes that don't fit the Kingdom—it isn't God. It's a voice from another source, a counterfeit bearing bad fruit. Knowing the difference will sharpen our hearing and keep our hearts and minds at peace.

Lord, help me recognize Your words by the environment they create within me. You may speak convicting, sobering words, but I know You will never oppress me with guilt, shame, fear, anxiety, or depression. Fill me with joy and peace, lift me up and inspire me, and give me rest with the sound of Your voice.

I am confident I will see the LORD's goodness

while I am here in the land of the living.

PSALM 27:13

*O*ne day, when the Lord returns . . ." These words have come off the lips of innumerable Christians when life in the present isn't quite working out. We tend to give up on the here and now and focus on the there and then. These words have an uncanny effect of sounding like a lament and a comfort simultaneously, and sometimes we're not sure which it is. But we know they signify some lack of satisfaction now.

These words are true, of course, but we tend to focus on "one day" much more often than Scripture does. Yes, it tells us of the coming Kingdom and describes a glorious end, but it also tells us the Kingdom has already come and that glory can be experienced now. Here, David expresses confidence that he will experience God's goodness in the land of the living—that is, in this age in this earthly realm. Life isn't all hardship, no matter how difficult our momentary circumstances might be. For David, and for us, there are tangible blessings to be discovered and received right now.

Much of the church has spent so much effort combating the health-and-wealth gospel that it has presented an opposite error: the suffering-and-poverty gospel. In truth, neither picture is biblical. We live in two realms simultaneously, and we experience the good and bad in both. And though we will encounter hardships in this world—Jesus assured us of that—we are nowhere told that we will encounter *only* hardships. We can come to God with the confident expectation that we will see His goodness here, now, and forever.

> *Lord, these are the ears I want to listen with—the attitude*
> *that assumes Your goodness will show up in every situation*
> *I face in every area of life. Your goodness is not a theory;*
> *it's real and tangible and evident. I'm grateful for that*
> *and fully expect to see it more.*

[Jesus said,] "The words I speak are not my own, but my Father

who lives in me does his work through me."

JOHN 14:10

From the Heart of God

"I have given you an example to follow. In human flesh, I said and did what I observed from the Father, who was living within Me. You, too, can do and say what you observe from the Holy Spirit who is living within you. When you are in fellowship with Me, the lines between us begin to blur. You will have difficulty knowing where you end and I begin, or vice versa. That's how it is in intimate relationships. The bond creates a unity that makes distinguishing the source of thoughts and desires extremely difficult—and completely unnecessary. When you live in closeness to Me, you can speak of many thoughts and desires as 'ours'—not yours or Mine, but ours. We live and breathe together.

"I have also given you a deep truth in this statement. I've shown you the unbreakable link between words and works. They aren't distinct, as if you can accept the words without living them out.

They are two sides of the same coin. To accept them is to live them; to live them is to accept them. Yes, plenty of people have mouthed My words without really embracing them, and as you know, this hypocrisy angers and disappoints Me. But their actions have clearly shown that they did not fully understand or accept the words. Those who truly believe I am Lord will do what I say because My words matter to them. They care for My heart.

"Let unity with Me be your goal. Don't seek to speak or follow either your words or My words as much as you seek to follow our words. My Spirit lives in you. Your life is not your own. We function together. I live in you and do My work in you, speaking through you, and to you, and for you. As you draw close to Me, you and I become we."

Jesus, I would love to know how You heard the Father and how He did His work in You. Show me how that works. Draw me into that kind of unity.

Jesus took them through the writings of Moses and all the prophets, explaining

from all the Scriptures the things concerning himself.

LUKE 24:27

*H*ebrew Scripture had been scrutinized for centuries. Some parts of it were older than others, but it had all been the subject of intense study among Jews long before the time of Jesus. Yet Jesus was somehow able to unveil meanings in Scripture that applied to Him and that no one had yet understood. The Messiah had been hinted at, symbolized, foreshadowed, and foretold for hundreds of years, but no one had seen Him clearly in God's Word. The plain meaning of the text had not been all that plain.

Many today argue that the meaning of Scripture is clear, and in many respects it is. God's plan of salvation and His general will for our lives are spelled out in simple terms. But when people argue that all the meaning is on the surface and urge others to quit looking for deeper truths, they are denying the layers in which God speaks. Rabbinic interpreters have long seen at least four approaches to the Word: (1) a literal, surface meaning; (2) a deeper meaning often found in hints and nuances of words;

(3) a metaphorical or allegorical meaning taken from symbolism in a passage; and (4) a hidden, subjective, mystical interpretation. Whether every passage is subject to all four approaches is open to discussion, but God has shown Himself capable of embedding truth at multiple levels in Scripture, which is why commentators are still uncovering the meaning of certain symbolic expressions in ancient texts. God's voice is able to express infinite truths in a finite number of words. He can creatively apply His words to a variety of situations at one time.

Always embrace the plain meaning of Scripture, but also hear God's voice between the lines, underneath the stories, through the symbols and images, and behind the printed words. He is communicating more than meets the eye.

> *Lord, heighten my senses to hear deeper truths, see bigger visions, and feel the weight of Your voice. Let Your Spirit explain the Scriptures to me personally and specifically.*

When he, the Spirit of truth, comes, he will guide you into all the truth.

JOHN 16:13, NIV

*W*e wish we could sit down with Jesus face-to-face and start firing questions at Him. Audible words, no ambiguity, just straightforward answers. But when Jesus spoke with His disciples on the night before His crucifixion, He assured them it would be better for Him to leave and for His Spirit to come dwell in them (John 16:7). Somehow the mystical relationship between His followers and His Spirit would be better than the manifest relationship they already had with Him. They would be better equipped to hear and handle truth.

It's hard for us to imagine that an inaudible voice would be a better guide for us than audible words straight from the Savior's mouth, but that's what Jesus said. The Spirit is a teacher, a counselor, a communicator. He doesn't just share information with us; He guides us into truth—the reality on which we can base our entire lives. When we know His truth—whether we understand it or not—making the right decisions becomes a lot less complicated. And when we don't know His truth for a specific situation, we can trust that He will lead us into it.

Our primary experience with the Godhead in this age is with the Holy Spirit. That's the relationship we need to cultivate. Any direct experience of God, whether of sensing His presence or hearing His voice, comes through the Spirit. The more we build that relationship, being sensitive to the ways He moves and the thoughts He fills us with, the more we will be able to hear God's words in any given situation. It's a long-term process, not a short-term transaction. When being continually filled with the Spirit becomes our highest pursuit, hearing God's voice becomes a regular experience.

> *Holy Spirit, fill me with Your thoughts, acquaint me with Your ways, saturate me with Your presence. Help me to hear Your voice as You breathe into me moment by moment.*

A voice from the cloud said, "This is my Son, my Chosen One. Listen to him."

LUKE 9:35

*J*esus and three of His disciples went up to a mountaintop to pray. As Jesus was praying, His appearance changed, Moses and Elijah appeared, a cloud descended, and God spoke. He singled out Jesus as the one to listen to. The shining representatives of the law and the prophets withdrew from the scene. The Son stood alone.

Jesus is the clearest, most direct voice of God in Scripture. It isn't that Moses' law or the prophetic declarations weren't also from God, but they weren't the ultimate revelation. They were not the words that would become the foundation of the Kingdom. They were directions, warnings, and glimpses of God's heart, but they weren't full expressions of the divine will. Jesus' words were somehow qualitatively different. They came not through the filter of a sinful human being's mouth or pen, but directly from the mouth of God incarnate. We must follow the instructions of the voice from heaven: listen to Him.

"Listen" in Scripture doesn't mean just to comprehend. It means to embrace or to heed. It implies not only that we hear what is said but that we also carry it out. As when an older adult admonishes a child to "listen to your parents," the goal isn't simply to hear. It's to take the message to heart and do something about it. Far too few Christians diligently *listen* to Jesus' words in Scripture. We admire them and honor them, but we often aren't zealous about following them. That has to change.

Never be on the lookout for God's voice of personal guidance if you aren't also on the lookout for God's voice in Jesus. When He says, "Love your neighbor as yourself," for example, He really means it. God doesn't expect you to become a legalistic Christian Pharisee, but He does expect you to embrace His heart as it is revealed in what Jesus said. In every way we can, we must listen to Him.

Jesus, I want Your words to carry full weight in my life. Let them sink deep into my heart. Let them become a part of who I am.

[Jesus said,] "Those the Father has given me will come to me,

and I will never reject them."

JOHN 6:37

John Bunyan was tormented by guilt. At times, he was comforted by the fact that the apostle Peter was forgiven for denying Christ. At other times, he was distraught over the fact that Esau was rejected even after turning back to the Lord and seeking Him. Was Bunyan a Peter or an Esau? A new creation or a blasphemous sinner? The torment continued until the assurance of Jesus' words sank into his heart: *He will never reject those who come to Him.*

Before his conversion, Bunyan understood the words of God simply as words. Scripture was a book of theological information. But after his conversion, the Bible came alive to him. God's voice was in it. He read Scripture with renewed zeal, its words now being the keys to the Kingdom, shining the truth and love of God on him with wonderful clarity. The Bible had not changed, but his relationship with the Author certainly had. What had once been a stale and condemning religious book became a source of life and fullness.

Many people read the Bible without ever hearing God's voice in it. Others read it with deep conviction that they are receiving the words of God straight from His mouth. What's the difference? Relationship. When we know the Father, we begin to see Him clearly in His Word as well as in our circumstances, the direction of our lives, and the people around us. What once appeared confusing and lifeless now overflows with goodness and blessing. God's voice becomes clear to those who know Him, and the better we get to know Him, the stronger our sense of it grows. When we look at the Bible, we may not grasp who Jesus is. But when we look at Jesus, we grasp everything His Word speaks to us.

Jesus, give me the gift of seeing Your Word with new eyes, as if I'm reading it for the first time every day. Make my vision come alive with new insights every time I gaze into the truth of Your Word.

DAY 23

"Abraham!" God called. "Yes," he replied. "Here I am."

GENESIS 22:1

*A*braham's hope in God's promise took a surprising and excruciating turn one day when God told him to take Isaac, the promised son, to a mountain and sacrifice him. God revealed this plan only after calling Abraham's name and hearing his response: "Here I am." It's a simple expression, used only a few times in Scripture. When used in conversation with God, it's an obedient response that always seems to have monumental consequences.

Jacob used this phrase twice: once when an angel spoke to him in a dream, which led to his return to the homeland and his name being changed to Israel; and once when Joseph was rediscovered in Egypt, which led to Israel's four hundred years there. Moses used it at the burning bush, which led to Israel's deliverance from Egypt. Samuel responded to God's call with that phrase and became the priestly prophet who would anoint Israel's first two kings. One of those kings, David, wrote a messianic verse that includes that phrase and declares the speaker to be "the one" written about in the scroll. The writer of Hebrews attributes this phrase prophetically to Jesus, the Messiah who saved humanity. And Isaiah spoke it when he encountered God's glory and heard the Lord ask, "Who will go for us?" In every case, major historical events turned on the response of "Here I am."

How would your life change if you said "Here I am" to God? You can't know for sure unless you do, but you wouldn't regret it. It might require laying down a dream or destiny you've long held tightly, but the cost pales in comparison to the blessing. God Himself spoke this phrase once—"When you call, the LORD will answer. 'Yes, I am here,' he will quickly reply"—about our salvation and healing coming quickly like the dawn (Isaiah 58:8-9). When we make ourselves completely available to God, He makes Himself completely available to us.

> *Lord, I present myself to You as a living sacrifice, whether history hinges on my commitment or not. I make this offering to You: to be moved and activated by Your voice. Here I am.*

DAY 24

During that time the devil came and said to [Jesus],

"If you are the Son of God . . ."

MATTHEW 4:3

A voice from heaven proclaimed, "This is my dearly loved Son." But no word from God goes uncontested, so Jesus was immediately led—by God's own Spirit—into the wilderness, where He would be tempted by Satan. We often see this encounter as a threefold temptation about turning stones into bread, jumping off the Temple, and winning the kingdoms of the world through false worship. But before the devil's first insidious prompt, an even greater temptation came: "If you are the Son of God . . ." It was a calculated strike against the identity that had just been declared. God said Jesus was His Son; the adversary responded, "Oh, really?"

That's an alarmingly accurate picture of the greatest temptations we will ever face. We may be preoccupied with greed, lust, pride, or whatever else, but we will find that the enemy of our souls has two very subtle weapons that are even more effective: (1) he undermines the identity we've already been given in Christ; and (2) he questions whatever God has just told us, daring us to actually believe it.

That's why anytime we learn a great new spiritual truth, we may soon find ourselves in a wilderness of contradiction that screams how untrue that truth actually is. Have you learned that you're seated with Christ in heavenly realms (Ephesians 2:6)? Circumstances may try to convince you that you are hopelessly earthbound. Have you read that you have authority over the power of the enemy (Luke 10:19)? Life seems to laugh at your impotence. Your response must be like that of Jesus: Cling firmly to what God has said. His voice is true. Faith will prove it—eventually. Your identity as His royal child will be confirmed, and so will all His promises. In the intensity of the battle, never let go of that.

Lord, the temptations are fierce. I know what You said, but I see so many contradictions. Give me the strength and the tenacity to hold on. I am who You say I am, and You will do what You said You will do.

Gideon said to God, "If you are truly going to use me to rescue Israel as you promised, prove it to me in this way. I will put a wool fleece on the threshing floor tonight. If the fleece is wet with dew in the morning but the ground is dry, then I will know that you are going to help me rescue Israel as you promised."

JUDGES 6:36-37

*G*ideon had already asked for a sign to make sure God was speaking to him (Judges 6:17). Here he asks for another sign to see if God's promise is true. And when God grants that request, Gideon will again ask for a sign to make sure the last one was accurate. His tentativeness may seem faithless to us, and perhaps it was. But God was patient with him and gave the reassurances he asked for. Gideon's repeated asking wasn't ideal, but neither was it sinful. When God calls people to a big assignment, he makes sure they get the message.

We sometimes hesitate to ask God for multiple confirmations, but then we question the two or three we've already received. We may look down on people who ask for signs, but then we proceed just as tentatively as Gideon would have without them.

We need to remember that God is patient with our attempts to hear His voice and follow Him, and He understands our uncertainties. He probably doesn't want us to keep asking after many confirmations—that would be an indication of unbelief—but He will give us enough clarity for us to anchor our faith in what He has said. He wants us to be confident in His words.

Don't be afraid to ask God for something concrete that would confirm His words. Don't depend on outward confirmations; He won't be backed into a corner and compelled to prove Himself. But give Him the opportunity to reassure you. And when He does, believe Him. He wants you to trust the direction He has given you.

Lord, I know we walk by faith and not by sight. But sometimes I need reassurance that my faith is heading in the right direction. Be patient with me. Show me signs, and give me faith to believe them.

He is always wrestling in prayer for you.

COLOSSIANS 4:12, NIV

A friend was at a dinner party when she suddenly felt an
urge to pray for her husband. He was away on a business trip in
Germany, and though there was no fear in her impulse to pray,
she sensed he needed the Holy Spirit's support. So she excused
herself from the table and interceded for him until she felt at
peace.

When she talked to her husband later, she understood why
the Spirit had prompted her to pray. At that moment, her husband and his traveling companions had been with a group of
businessmen who were pressing them to visit the city's infamous
red-light district for an evening of entertainment. They were
steadfastly resisting, but the businessmen were stubbornly insist-
ing. Eventually, the visitors' refusal trumped the hosts' insistence,
and the plans were abandoned. The Spirit provided strength in a
time of need.

God often impresses us to intercede for people in danger
or distress. Some people who are sensitive to the Holy Spirit
wake up in the middle of the night with a sudden urge to pray

for a missionary or relative halfway around the world, finding out only later what the urgent need was about. Regardless of why these prayers are necessary for God to accomplish His will, they are apparently effective. Many crises, temptations, and evil threats have been averted at the precise moment when someone prayed without knowing exactly why.

Don't resist sudden urges to pray for someone. If these urges are motivated by fear or panic, they almost certainly aren't the Holy Spirit's prompting; but if motivated by an awareness of intense need, they almost certainly are. Those who are sensitive to these burdens will be called on to intercede at critical moments. And their strategic prayers will greatly influence the Kingdom, even halfway around the world.

Holy Spirit, I would love to be a reliable intercessor in moments of need. Sensitize me to the impressions and burdens You give. I don't need to understand why; *I need only to know* when *You want me to pray, and I will respond with zeal.*

Jesus replied, "All who love me will do what I say. My Father will love them,

and we will come and make our home with each of them."

JOHN 14:23

From the Heart of God

"How would you feel if you had a friend who listened to your advice but never really acted on it? How would you feel if your most heartfelt words were neglected or casually dismissed? Would you take it personally? Most people would, and understandably so. Your thoughts and feelings are expressed in words, and when your words are ignored, it hurts. They represent who you are. And when someone takes them seriously enough to act on them, you feel valued.

"Many people say they love Me but don't demonstrate that they value Me by keeping My words. It's possible to do what I say without loving Me, but it isn't possible to love Me without doing what I say. Those who disregard My words don't really value them or understand My heart. Those who want to know Me and love who I am will also embrace wholeheartedly what I say. Your response to My words is a revealing picture of what you think and how you feel about Me.

"My heart warms when you embrace My words. The Father and I love you at all times, regardless of how you respond to Us, but Our love for you swells with joy when you honor Us, want to become like Us, and are eager to do what We say. I have drawn you into a relationship not only so you can know My love but also so I can know yours. The substance of My instructions is important—I want you to follow My words—but it is much less important than the love your response reveals. I'm much more interested in your heart than your obedience. But show Me your heart by what you do."

Jesus, forgive me for assuming I can love You in attitude without loving You in action. I love this promise—that You and the Father will come and make Your home with me. Please do so. I want You to feel at home in my heart.

God knows how much I [Paul] love you and long for you

with the tender compassion of Christ Jesus.

PHILIPPIANS 1:8

I felt an overwhelming surge of compassion for the woman I'd just met, and I didn't even know why. I didn't know her story—nothing about her needs, experiences, problems, or relationships. Her expression may have subtly revealed some discouragement, but there was no striking indication that she needed sympathy. I simply felt compassion. And I had an almost irresistible urge to act on it.

Sometimes we sense God's emotions for someone else. When we can't put our finger on why we feel encouraged, loving, concerned, joyful, or anything else that might come from God's heart, we may be picking up what is actually in His heart for that person. An unexplained sense of anger, condemnation, or judgment may come from an entirely different source, but God's compassion flows through His people toward others. Why? So that we'll act on those impulses and show His compassion. He wants us to represent His goodness to the world, and sudden shifts in emotions or attitudes may be a divine nudge to display what's in His heart.

Don't assume that all feelings are simply your own. If you are a vessel of the Spirit's presence, it only makes sense that He would move you through His desires and attitudes. He is a ministering, missionary Spirit who wants to draw people to the Father through the Son and lavish His goodness on His people. Any urge to bless likely comes from the influence of God's Spirit in your heart. It may be there simply for your awareness, but more often it's there to move you to some sort of expression or action. The tender compassion of Christ—as well as His encouragement, His favor, His forgiveness, and more—is on display in His people.

Jesus, I long to express Your heart to people. Help me recognize the movement of Your Spirit within me—the swells and impulses and attitudes—and give me opportunities to respond to them. Put Your heart on display in me.

> *[Rebekah] went to ask the LORD about it.*
>
> *"Why is this happening to me?" she asked.*
>
> *And the LORD told her.*
>
> GENESIS 25:22-23

*R*ebekah had questions for God. So did Job, who didn't understand what God was doing in his life. So did Habakkuk, whose prophecy starts with a series of questions that sound a bit accusatory regarding God's fairness. Many others in Scripture and throughout history have been bold enough to bring their most pointed questions to God, expecting a response. Sometimes they got answers, sometimes they didn't, and sometimes their attitudes were corrected. But God never rebuked them simply for asking.

If we want to hear God, we need to ask Him questions. Most of us do that indirectly—sometimes tentatively, hoping for guidance and direction, and sometimes with hints of complaint, wondering why He isn't doing what we want Him to do. But asking God specific questions with the expectation that He will respond to us is an act of faith. We can ask Him what His desires are, how He sees us, how He sees others, how He feels about this situation or that problem, how He wants our relationship to develop, how He wants us to see things differently, what He wants to teach us, and much, much more. These questions may include guidance and specific requests, but they go well beyond those concerns and delve into the heart of the relationship. And God invites us into that kind of conversation. He wants to be known. Questions that open our hearts for Him to share Himself are always welcome.

When we do this in an attitude of faith and expectation, we begin to see and hear things we didn't notice before. Divine moments of instruction—"aha" moments that unveil His nature—come much more frequently. We begin to feel God's heartbeat and synchronize with it. We become not just hearers of God's voice but conversationalists with God Himself.

Lord, what is on Your heart today? What do You want to teach me? My eyes and ears are open—please share Your heart with me.

I am the LORD who brought you out of Ur of the Chaldeans

to give you this land as your possession.

GENESIS 15:7

The man's business was going well, even growing, and the future seemed bright. But one day he heard God tell him to hold a going-out-of-business sale and close his doors. On the surface, it seemed like bad advice, and his wife thought so too. Surely this couldn't be God's will. Maybe the man had misheard. But God doesn't give bad advice, and sometimes His voice can't be so easily dismissed as a misunderstanding. This word was clear. So the man went out of business and, in the painful aftermath, remained unemployed for a year.

What went wrong? Had God misled him? No, after a year of second-guessing God, he saw how the Lord began to provide new opportunities. The career change ended up being one of the best things that ever happened to this couple. They have prospered ever since. But it wasn't easy at first. Following God rarely is. It takes time to see the fruits of obedience.

This is a common theme in Scripture. God called Abraham to leave home and go to a land He would show him later.

Abraham had plenty of opportunities to second-guess his decision to follow—his wife was even captured at one point—but God eventually vindicated his faith. Plenty of other people in the Bible were led in seemingly absurd directions, yet following always proved to be the right thing to do. That's what life is like when you believe God speaks. He leads in ways that, on the surface, don't always make sense.

But His ways do make sense, and eventually we are able to see how. Hearing and responding to His voice is a real possibility. Others may question our hearing, but their voices aren't the ones we follow. We follow God into whatever land He shows us.

Lord, if You will speak to me clearly, I'll go in any direction You tell me, regardless of what other people think about it or how much sense it makes to me at the time. My steps belong to You.

Trust in the LORD with all your heart;

do not depend on your own understanding.

PROVERBS 3:5

Some people suggest that many Christians spend too much time trying to discern God's "perfect will" rather than simply following the heart and wisdom God gave them. The assumption behind this suggestion is that God doesn't have a single-minded purpose for us but allows us a range of choices. And if a big purchase or a geographic move or a marriage partner seems okay to us, why not feel the freedom to take a major step without hearing from God about it?

There's a kernel of truth in this argument—God does put desires and wisdom into our hearts—but not enough truth to make this the prevailing pattern for our lives. Especially in major decisions, God loves to speak to us and guide us. In fact, Proverbs urges us to forsake our own understanding as we seek God's direction. Why? Because God's will often runs contrary to our own thought processes. From a human point of view, He led Abraham, Joseph, Moses, Joshua, the prophets, and many others in absolutely ludicrous directions. Why, then, would we abandon our attempts to hear His voice and make His guidance a matter within our own minds? That's the solution of a generation that doesn't have the patience or yearning to press in and wait for God to speak, no matter how long it takes or how much deeper into His presence He calls us. That's the advice of an impatient spirit that doesn't believe God speaks very often. And it isn't very biblical.

Scripture is filled with specific guidance from the voice of God, and it presents the possibility of hearing Him not as a rare exception but as a normal lifestyle. We have a tremendous capacity for making wrong decisions, and when we look in the rearview mirror, we often wish we had gotten clearer guidance. If we will be patient and persistent in seeking God's direction, that guidance will come.

Lord, I don't want to just do whatever seems right. My understanding is limited, but You know what's best. I want to hear You clearly and specifically.

DAY 32

God is making his appeal through us. We speak for Christ

when we plead, "Come back to God!"

2 CORINTHIANS 5:20

*J*esus is the Word of God, the *logos* behind all of creation, and the written Word is His revelation. So why would God need us to be His mouthpieces? Because He's an infinite God, and He needs an infinite number of stories if He wants to demonstrate the many facets of His nature. That's one of the reasons He created billions of bearers of His image. We all have the potential to uniquely represent something about God that others cannot. He reveals Himself through a multitude of stories, and each of ours is one of them.

So we make appeals as if we were the voice of Christ, pleading with people to be reconciled to God. We not only speak His message to them; we embody it. We are living testimonies of what Christ has done, examples of His ability to resurrect, heal, redeem, restore, call, and equip. We are stories of His provision, protection, comfort, guidance, and promises. We teach, preach, and live His words. We are a vast multitude of vessels, carrying His presence and His voice into every corner of this world.

Does that sound too ambitious or presumptuous? Regardless of how it sounds, it's true. God has made it clear that His glory will cover the earth, and He does hardly anything on earth that doesn't involve His people. When His glory covers the earth, it will largely be through us. When He speaks, it has almost always come through a prophetic voice or a testimony or a written record of His ways—all inspired by His Spirit but made manifest through a human agent. We need to remember our sacred role. We not only hear and receive God's voice; we are called to express it everywhere we can.

> *Lord, my story doesn't seem very dramatic or impressive. Yet I know Your hand has been deeply involved in writing it. Therefore, it reveals something about You. May I never be guilty of hiding or minimizing Your glory in my story. I share You well by sharing who I am.*

You are a chosen people. You are royal priests,

a holy nation, God's very own possession.

1 PETER 2:9

*T*his statement from Peter is either true or (as far as we know) potentially true of everyone we meet. Even the most hardened criminal or twisted psychopath is a candidate to become a chosen, royal priest and a child of God. But in attempting to share God's Word, many Christians focus on the sin in people's lives. Some of us have a tendency to point out where others are falling short of God's standards. We don't focus on their potential in God's Kingdom; we focus on their experience outside of it.

That isn't God's voice. It's true that the Spirit convicts of sin, but He rarely needs us to help with that. We aren't called to point out each other's faults. No, when God speaks through us to other members or potential members of His body, the voice is not condemning. It's full of hope. We are to see the treasure He has put in others and to call it out. If we ask God how He sees the people around us, He will show us His love for them and what they will look like in Christ. He will point out their gifts or their fruitfulness in the Kingdom. He doesn't reveal what we have no business knowing. He urges us to bless the good that He is cultivating in others.

Paul told the Corinthians that prophetic ministry among believers is for strengthening, encouraging, and comforting (1 Corinthians 14:3). If you're sensitive to the Spirit, that's what you'll hear: words that build up and bring hope. Ask God what's on His heart that He wants to share with others, and He will give you glimpses of the treasure He has placed within them. And you will be able to affirm what He wants to do in their lives.

Lord, give me hope-filled words. Show me the treasure in Your people. Let me see them through spiritual eyes and bless what You are doing in their lives.

I tell you the truth, the Son can do nothing by himself. He does only what he

sees the Father doing. Whatever the Father does, the Son also does.

JOHN 5:19

Some people see Jesus as the exception. Others see Him as their example. Though it's true He is rather exceptional, He came to us as a human being to show us how we are to live and relate to the Father. Philippians 2:6-7 says that Jesus gave up the privileges of deity to live among us, meaning that He shows us what is possible for us if we live in perfect obedience to God's Spirit. So, if the Son can do nothing by Himself but only does what He sees the Father doing, what does that say about us? We, too, are meant to do nothing independently, but to follow the lead of the Father. We are to listen to Him and respond as a way of life.

How can we see what the Father is doing? We have to learn to notice what He's doing, where He's working, and when He's setting up a situation for His glory. That might sound hard, but it really isn't if we ask Him to heighten our spiritual senses to His activity. He will alert us to His presence, His work, and His words as we choose to consciously watch and listen. Every time we ask, "Lord, where are You in this situation? What are You up to?" He will answer by speaking deep in our hearts or making His movements clear. Because He wants us to live with constant awareness of Him, He will make constant awareness a real possibility.

Become a *noticer*. Ask the Father what He's up to. Watch where He's working. Align yourself with His activity and do what you see Him doing. Hearing His voice isn't nearly as difficult when we're aware of His activity and partnering with Him in it.

> *Lord, imitation may be the sincerest form of flattery, but it's also the sincerest form of worship I can offer You. Heighten my spiritual senses to recognize Your footprint everywhere You go so I can do what You're doing.*

DAY 35

Ask the LORD your God for a sign of confirmation.

ISAIAH 7:11

$\mathcal{A}$ situation I had been praying about took a sudden turn for the worse. I was confused and more than a little distressed. Why was God not answering my prayers? Why would He allow this problem to come up? Didn't He care about the situation? I got in my car to drive home, pleading with Him—even arguing with Him—about the injustice of the situation. And when I pulled into the garage and stopped, I looked down at the mileage marker above my odometer—the four-digit counter for tracking trips. It stood at a number that had already been very significant in the situation, a number that had been tied to the victim of the injustice in several ways. God was reminding me that He was still on top of the situation, no matter how it looked.

Many would regard my seeing that number as a coincidence, but in context, it wasn't. The odds of seeing that four-digit number at any given moment were one in ten thousand, and it happened to be at an exact moment when I was distraught and praying about the situation. To a casual observer, it's random. To someone crying out to God, it's His voice.

God is the master of all circumstances, and there are no real coincidences in His Kingdom. Yes, life functions by the laws of physics that God has put in place, but He has a way of timing occurrences to speak through them, especially to those who are carrying on a conversation with Him. When we ask Him for encouragement or confirmation, we are negligent not to receive it when He gives it. And giving it through an outward sign has significant biblical precedents. God doesn't want us to depend on outward signs, but He certainly allows us to receive confirmation through them. He speaks through the events He orchestrates—even the seemingly random ones.

Lord, make me attentive to the signs and symbols around me. Draw my eyes to what I need to see. Let the world around me— and the events You orchestrate—become an integral part of our conversations.

[Jesus said,] "I have given you an example to follow.

Do as I have done to you."

JOHN 13:15

From the Heart of God

"You want specific direction for your life, and I am glad to give it. My sheep hear My voice—I make sure of it. All they need to do is keep listening and learning. But in all your attempts to get guidance from Me and to learn about your future, I want you to realize how much I've already told you. Remember that My priority for you is for you to know Me, to be filled with Me, to become like Me. Yes, I want to direct what you do, but I'm more concerned about *who you are*. If I am your source of life—not just by creation, but by your constant dependence on Me—what you do will become clear enough. Your heart is the bigger issue.

"Do you realize how much I've already spoken to you? My example is My word, My illustration for who and what you are to become. In every act, in every word, in every expression of compassion or love or anger, I have demonstrated My will for your life. Just as I looked to the Father and did only what I saw Him doing, I want you to look to Me as your template for life. You can love as I love, feel as I feel, think as I think, and act as I act. Everything I did, I did as a human being depending on the Father and the Spirit. I did not invoke My divine privileges. That would have made Me an exception you could never emulate, not an example you could follow. I intend for you to understand everything you hear Me saying as My words for you. Love what I love, hate what I hate, act as I act, speak as I speak. This is My will for your life."

Jesus, help me to not only listen for the messages You speak, but also to hear the messages You've already given. I can't be like You unless You pour Your life into me. Empower me to do what I see You doing.

[God said,] "Now I will tell you new things, secrets you have not yet heard."

ISAIAH 48:6

*L*ord, teach me something about You that I don't already know."
This request of mine was answered when I overheard my wife
talking to my son. He had been anxious about a health issue,
and he needed reassurance. Lots of it. Again and again. And he
kept asking to be reminded that he would be okay. Finally, my
wife said, "Saying it again isn't going to make it any more true
than it was the first time I told you."

Immediately, I saw myself in that verbal exchange. I had
been anxious about a problem and asking God for reassurance.
Lots of it. Again and again. And He had given me plenty of
encouragement to believe what I already knew to be true. Yet my
heart was anxious, and I kept feeling the need to hear His confirmation time after time. He let me know His perspective on my
neediness through my wife's words to my son. Hearing it from
God again wasn't going to make it any more true than the first
time I heard Him. When He says something, it's true—without
an expiration date.

Asking God to teach us something we don't already know

or that we need to understand better is always a welcome question. He loves to show us new things, and He will open our eyes to illustrations and parables around us to display who He is. When we're focused on learning about God rather than on self-improvement, failures, needs, and desires, we grow in the relationship and are transformed without even being aware of it. As in any relationship, greater intimacy cultivates greater sensitivity and conformity to the other's interests. When we ask God to show us more of Himself, He finds a way to speak to our hearts and draw us closer.

> *Lord, I long to know who You are—deeply, intimately, and beyond religious explanations. And I know You are zealous to unveil Your nature personally to those who long for You. Give me pictures of Your perspective so I can know Your heart.*

Everyone spoke well of [Jesus] and was amazed

by the gracious words that came from his lips.

LUKE 4:22

𝓙esus visited His hometown synagogue and read the weekly Scripture passage for the Sabbath gathering. Then He sat down—probably in the "Moses seat" from which the sermon was normally delivered—and added some commentary implying that He was the fulfillment of the verses he had just read, found in Isaiah 61:1-2. His audience couldn't have fully understood the implications, but they understood enough to marvel that this son of a carpenter was speaking knowledgeably and eloquently on prophetic Scriptures. They found His words to be gracious and surprising.

That's one way we can recognize the voice of God. Thoughts that come from His Spirit are fresh and inspiring. Some people marvel at how sharp and creative they are when they have new insights, but most of us realize we aren't as brilliant as we'd like to think we are. We know we have a deep well of revelation to draw from, and it isn't anything we ourselves could produce. It has been put into us by the Holy Spirit, who has far greater wisdom and understanding than we have. When those gracious, inspiring, and surprising thoughts come to the surface, they must be from Him.

Ask God to give you unexpected insights. Ask for illustrations, parables, connecting ideas, and angles on biblical passages that you haven't seen before. Pray as Paul did that the eyes of your heart would be flooded with light so you can rise to new levels of wisdom and understanding (Ephesians 1:17-18). Learn to recognize sudden ideas and inspiration not as products of your own mind but of the Spirit who lives within you. And thank Him for the gracious words He has poured into your life and will continue to speak in the days and years to come.

Jesus, Your words are truth. I expect them to stretch me, inspire me, fill me with hope, and counsel me with deeper wisdom than I have on my own. Give me fresh ideas and insights. With the ears of my heart, help me recognize the words You speak.

DAY 39

This is the sign from the LORD to prove that he will do as he promised: I will

cause the sun's shadow to move ten steps backward on the sundial of Ahaz!

ISAIAH 38:7-8

*L*ord, if I'm believing in the wrong thing and heading in the wrong direction—I'll walk away. Just speak to me clearly. But if You want me to press ahead, show me the sign I'm looking for." I prayed that prayer on a discouraging day when I was headed out the door for a walk. The sign I was looking for—cardinals— was a common symbol to me. God had spoken to me this way before, the cardinal representing hope and promise. The more I saw, the greater the affirmation. Where I live, seeing one cardinal isn't unusual, but the timing in my conversations with God has been uncanny. In desperate times, they've flown over my head, landed on branches in front of me, and seemingly stared at me as if God were delivering a personal message. I believed He had spoken this way many times; and on this day, I desperately needed another bit of confirmation.

By the end of my walk, I had seen nine cardinals (and nine happened to be a symbolic number in the situation I was pray- ing about). The most I had ever seen on that route was four, and usually it was one or two at the most. Very often I would see none. But on this day, right after I said, "Lord, I'll take any cardinals as affirmation to continue in the direction I've been going," I saw them flying across my path, landing in the bushes next to the path, darting over my head, and perched on branches above, chirping emphatically. Just as Hezekiah asked for and received a sign with the sun in Isaiah 38, I asked for a sign with one particular bird. And the God who orchestrates His creation gave it to me.

> *Lord, I know You often choose not to speak this way, and I can't assume that the absence of a sign means no. It may simply mean You want to speak another way. But when You do speak this way, it is so very encouraging. Thank You for designing well-orchestrated "coincidences."*

DAY 40

Come to me with your ears wide open. Listen, and you will find life.

ISAIAH 55:3

*C*hristians are fond of quoting the Bible as God's Word. We believe it is the collection of writings in which the God of the universe has revealed Himself. It tells of people's encounters with God, quotes prophets who heard Him, relates the story of His Son coming into this world and dying on our behalf, and testifies to the miracles of God's intervention in human lives. This book is a supernaturally inspired unveiling of ultimate reality.

This is an honorable belief; but when we admit that we haven't actually read the whole thing, it's also a hollow belief. Do we really value knowing God through His Word? Getting a glimpse behind the veil of the physical world? Hearing the divine voice and feeling the divine heartbeat? Walking in the wisdom rooted in eternity? Apparently not as much as we say we do. Surveys indicate that most Christians spend precious little time in the life-giving Scriptures or even asking God what He wants to say to us.

Why do we keep our distance from His voice? Perhaps we don't expect to hear Him or understand what He says, or we don't trust that what we heard was actually from Him. Or maybe we're afraid He will say things we don't want to hear—words of correction or rebuke or demands that will require time and energy on our part. But if we come with ears wide open, we won't be discouraged or humiliated by what we hear; we'll find life. His words will breathe energy into us. They will give us hope, not obligations; constructive advice, not destructive rebuke; opportunities and promises, not limitations and denials. Our days tend to suck the life out of us, but coming to God with open ears infuses life back into us. If we listen, we will find the supernatural support we need.

Father, Your Word is more than truth; it is life. Why would I ever neglect it or, worse yet, hide from it? I have nothing to fear in what You say and everything to gain. My ears are open; speak life to me.

DAY 41

The LORD had said to Abram, "Leave your native country, your relatives,

and your father's family, and go to the land that I will show you."

GENESIS 12:1

$\mathcal{W}$e long for more details. All we're told is that "the LORD had said to Abram." There's nothing about what the voice sounded like or how Abram heard it. Was it in a dream? Did it thunder from the sky? Was it the subtle impressions of a heart seeking God? We don't know. Why didn't God tell us more so we could listen for His words more specifically?

Perhaps He withheld the specifics because of what we usually do with them. Whenever we see details in Scripture, we tend to make templates out of them. We establish principles and then develop a relationship with the principles rather than with God. Then we fail to see anything outside "the norm" as genuine—even though God is almost always outside the norm. So the Bible describes a variety of modes of hearing God, and sometimes it simply tells us that He spoke and tantalizes us with the lack of specifics. We are left with nothing but our hunger to know what He is saying—which is likely exactly what He intends.

84

Those of us who want to hear God cannot afford to limit our attention to one mode of expression. Perhaps He will speak through the words of a friend, draw our attention to specific scriptural passages with a divine magnifying glass, or align circumstances in a way that confirms the inclinations of our Spirit-led hearts. More likely, He will reach out to us in a combination of expressions that complement each other and serve to strengthen our faith in Him. Then we can move forward confidently, knowing that the God who governs every detail of our lives is speaking through them and leading us to the places He will show us as we go.

Lord, I'm listening for You in whatever ways You want to speak. Please draw my attention to the messages You want me to notice. Let me hear Your singular direction from multiple angles so I can believe it's Your will.

DAY 42

Your sons and daughters will prophesy. Your young men will see visions,

and your old men will dream dreams.

ACTS 2:17

*O*n the day of Pentecost, when God poured out His Spirit on all the believers who were gathered, Peter quoted the prophet Joel about the "last days." But clearly, Peter wasn't talking about some future end-times era. He was pointing to that very day as the fulfillment of Joel's word. The clear implication is that the people of God were entering a time in which men, women, and children of all ages would be able to hear from God themselves. Their encounters with Him would include visions, dreams, and other prophetic sensitivities. God would no longer have to speak through a small group of prophets and priests. He would speak to them directly.

If that was true during Peter's days, and Joel called them the "last" or "latter" days, then we must still be living in that era. There have been varying degrees of the Holy Spirit's activity in church history; sometimes He moves in dramatic ways, and sometimes we have seemed to live in spiritual dark ages. But His gifts have always been fully available since Pentecost, and so has His voice. Ever since the Holy Spirit came to live inside God's new creation—this means anyone who belongs to Christ, according to 2 Corinthians 5:17—all things are possible. God is accessible. No one has to say, "Know the Lord," because all are able to know Him already (Jeremiah 31:34; Hebrews 8:11). He is no longer an obscure God.

It's true that we go through dark and confusing times when God seems to be silent, but it's important to know these are temporary, not normal conditions. Over time, God means for us to know Him. We must pray, pursue, and press in to Him, but He will make it happen. We live in an age of open communication with the divine.

> *Spirit of God, I long for clearer expressions of Your truth. Let me see visions and dream dreams, whatever that looks like and however You want to shape them. May the free-flowing spiritual environment of Pentecost be a reality in my life today.*

DAY 43

The LORD gave the donkey the ability to speak. "What have I done to you that deserves your beating me three times?" it asked Balaam. . . . Then the LORD opened Balaam's eyes, and he saw the angel of the LORD standing in the roadway with a drawn sword in his hand.

NUMBERS 22:28, 31

*B*alaam knew that God was not going to let him prophesy a curse against Israel, as the Moabite king had hired him to do, but he went out to Israel anyway. The donkey he rode could see an angel blocking the roadway, so it stopped, only to suffer the wrath of the misguided prophet. Finally, after the donkey had endured several beatings, God opened the animal's mouth. And after a brief and strange conversation between man and beast, God opened Balaam's eyes to see the angel too. God went to extreme measures to get the attention of the stubborn prophet.

Yes, God can speak through anything, even a donkey. It's easy to view this story as a myth or fable, though we often forget that the infinite God who created the universe can do anything He wants at any time through any means. If He can speak the world into being by the sound of His voice, everything else is simple.

A donkey talking for a few seconds? Not a problem. And more than a little humorous.

Never have contempt for the crude messengers in your life. We strain to hear God's voice through a high-profile speaker or a powerful and popular book, but He often tests us to see if we will also hear Him through that awkward misfit in the congregation or a grossly misspelled quote on Facebook. If we tune out the unlikely, we are unlikely to hear Him even in the obvious—as quite a few people in and around Bethlehem and Galilee found out during the time of Christ. The medium isn't the issue; the voice is. Listen *everywhere*.

Lord, there is no such thing as "unlikely" with You. I don't care to be impressed by the medium. I simply need You. Test my hearing however You choose—even if You have to open the mouth of a beast.

DAY 44

I also pray that you will understand the incredible

greatness of God's power for us who believe him.

EPHESIANS 1:19

*W*hen we listen for God's voice, we generally listen to Him with limited expectations. We don't mean to; we just don't know how to open ourselves to anything and everything. We need context, so we create one. But it's often a narrower context than it ought to be. Like a radio receiver tuned to one station, we rule out all other signals. We place limits on what we think we might hear. And if God speaks outside of those limits, we may miss His message.

Paul's prayer in Ephesians 1 is meant to raise our expectations. It pleads for wisdom and revelation to enlighten us and convince us of hope. In verse 19, it expands our vision to know a God who can do the impossible through those who believe Him. In effect, it asks God to build a greenhouse in our souls where His word is cultivated and blossoms. When we are convinced that God's power is available to us through faith, our faith is able to grasp greater possibilities. When we listen for His voice, we pray with more boldness. We look forward to miraculous answers. And we learn to expect the unexpected.

If we would pray Paul's prayer for ourselves daily, we would not only grow dramatically in our knowledge of God and in our relationship with Him, but we would also hear Him more clearly. The soil of our hearts would be better prepared for the seeds He wants to plant there. Our capacity for envisioning God's will would expand to accommodate the great things He wants to do. And we would begin to step more fully into the plans He has for us.

God, help me to understand the incredible greatness of Your power—not just in theory but in every way it applies to my life. I want to walk in Your strength. I want my heart to be big enough for Your purposes. Please let me hear all You want to say.

DAY 45

From eternity to eternity I am God. No one can snatch anyone

out of my hand. No one can undo what I have done.

ISAIAH 43:13

From the Heart of God

"I want you to understand all that 'from eternity to eternity' includes. It means that not only can no one undo anything I have done, but that no one can undo what I have *said*, either. It's true that I often interact with My people with a softness in My will; like Moses, you can change My direction with your prayers and pleas. And, also like Moses, you can forfeit promises that might have applied to you if you had been careful to believe and follow Me closely. But when I have spoken My promises and purposes to you, and you have believed them and been careful to align your life with them, you never need to worry about losing what was promised. No matter how things look, My words will come to pass. Whatever circumstances or arguments come up against them, no matter how unlikely My words may seem, they cannot be quenched or deferred by outside interference. The things I have spoken to you are a sacred trust, and you can hang on to them relentlessly and without fear.

"This may be hard for you to grasp, because you don't know anyone else whose words are unfailing. In the world, you can never be certain that people are able or willing to keep their word. But I am always able, and I would not have spoken My words if I had not been willing. I see the end from the beginning, and I would know if I were giving you false hope. When I speak hope into your life, that hope is real. It is certain. Hang on to it as the voice of an infinite, all-powerful God who cannot fail. You can listen well only when you remember this about Me and cling to who I am."

Eternal God, I'm so used to human wisdom that I forget how eternal and invincible Your words are. Help my spirit to get a true sense of their weight, and forgive me whenever my heart questions Your faithfulness. Nothing and no one can alter what You've spoken.

The angel of the LORD appeared to him in a

blazing fire from the middle of a bush.

EXODUS 3:2

*T*here are times in Scripture when God speaks so clearly and unmistakably that the hearer has no questions about His will. Those times are rare and generally reserved for major events in salvation history and for people with critical prophetic roles. But in discerning the varying degrees of intensity of God's voice in Scripture (He subtly whispers at some times and announces emphatically at others) we notice an interesting dynamic: The more clearly He speaks, the greater the demand for obedience.

Moses had few options. He tried to dissuade God from His plan, but God left him with no alternatives. There was no mistaking the words, no confusion about the instructions, no wiggle room at all. If Moses had decided not to go back into Egypt, he would not be able to claim that he misunderstood or that the voice wasn't clear. He would have had to willfully rebel.

Many of us say we long to hear God more clearly, but do we really? The clearer the revelation, the greater the expectations that come along with it. We can't hope for a clear direction from God and then consider whether we will follow it. When He speaks emphatically and unmistakably, it's usually because He is putting us in situations in which the temptation to flee will be great. There's a reason Moses saw a burning bush and heard God's voice audibly; his calling was dreadfully dangerous and intimidating. There's a reason Mary was visited by an angel; carrying a child out of wedlock was treacherous business. If we want this degree of hearing, we are also asking for this degree of responsibility. And it isn't as delightful as we might think.

Yearn for God's voice, but make no mistake about what the yearning will lead to: greater hearing and, therefore, much greater responsibility. An exceptional encounter with God demands stepping into an exceptional destiny.

Lord, I know the costs of hearing You are high, but I still want to encounter You. I am willing to face the responsibility of knowing Your will.

How good is a timely word!

PROVERBS 15:23, NIV

A member of our group asked for prayer for her mother, who was suffering from a terminal disease and increasingly unable to walk. Several times a day, her mother stumbled and fell, and the family would rush to her side. Mother, daughter, and everyone else in the family needed God's support.

After we prayed, we read through a preselected psalm, Psalm 145, with each person reading two verses aloud. When it came to the woman who had requested prayer for her mother, she began reading the verses that fell to her in the rotation: "The LORD upholds all who fall and lifts up all who are bowed down" (Psalm 145:14, NIV). She barely finished the words as the tears began to fall. God had directly acknowledged a personal need and promised to walk with this family through their trial.

God is the master of timely words. He knows the seating order of a group before they sit down and read. He knows years in advance which Bible passages and which devotionals will be read on a certain day, and He has a supernatural ability to coordinate them to speak directly into the events and issues of the reader's life. He knows how to direct us out of our normal patterns to listen to a message, read a passage of a book, or even overhear a casual comment that speaks profoundly into our hearts' desperate needs. He knows how to time His voice to get our attention and fit our circumstances.

Never hesitate to ask God for timely words. When you're discouraged, ask Him for encouragement. It always comes, usually sooner rather than later. When you need guidance or wisdom, ask Him to express His will in the messages you will hear through your conversations, readings, and exposure to His Word. Whatever your need, He has something to say. And He knows the perfect timing to say it.

> *Lord, impress upon me the folly of seeing timely words as "coincidences." You are the Master of my circumstances, and Your timing is impeccable. You coordinate the things I hear and see. Help me recognize Your voice in them.*

DAY 48

You are blessed because you believed that the Lord would do what he said.

LUKE 1:45

Nearly every Christian affirms a strong belief that God will do what He said He will do—that He will keep His promises, fulfill the blessings described in His Word, and prove Himself faithful and true in our lives. Yet if we're honest, in the back of our minds is a very subtle doubt, an "I hope so" or a "we'll see" that undermines the fullness of our faith. That's okay; God understands. When a man told Jesus he believed, while also asking Jesus to help his unbelief (Mark 9:24), Jesus followed through with a miracle. But that isn't ideal. Jesus also gave promises about prayer that were conditioned on not doubting (Matthew 21:21), and He marveled at His disciples' unbelief in the midst of storms (Mark 4:40). His desire is for us to believe He will do what He said. And His blessing is often reserved only for those who believe.

That's hard for us to swallow. We don't want God's blessings to depend on the purity of our faith, but some of them are. The size of our faith doesn't seem to be an issue; all we need is faith the size of a mustard seed (Matthew 17:20). But the quality of our faith may certainly have an effect on what we receive from God. Several passages of Scripture urge that our faith should not be mixed with doubt. He saves some of His most precious blessings for those who believe He will give them.

Elizabeth blessed Mary because Mary believed God would do what He said. Many people wouldn't have believed, finding the angel's words too bizarre to be literally true. But Mary accepted them, and Elizabeth expressed a profound biblical principle when she saw her. Just as Abraham was declared righteous because He believed God's impossible words, Mary was declared blessed because she believed Him too. Those who trust God's extraordinary words will find Him extraordinarily faithful.

> *Lord, I believe. If You said it, it's always true, no matter how strange or unlikely it seems. I accept Your ability to do the impossible, and I gratefully receive the blessing that comes through believing.*

DAY 49

This hope will not lead to disappointment.

ROMANS 5:5

*I*t's okay. You can allow yourself to hope. Not many people believe that. Or perhaps it would be more accurate to suggest that not many people believe they can hope for anything other than their ultimate salvation in Christ. But our hope in God is far more comprehensive than "someday in heaven." He has given us everything pertaining to life and godliness and access to His "great and precious promises" (2 Peter 1:3-4). Like David, we can be confident that we will see God's goodness in the land of the living (Psalm 27:13). He fills our lives not only with big-picture hope, but also day-to-day hope. He is the giver of every good gift.

Many people who listen for God's voice are predisposed to hearing His restrictions, limitations, and corrections. They may expect His encouragement to maintain hope for eternity but not for current situations. Yet God is far more willing to encourage us about today's circumstances than we think He is. He has solutions we haven't yet discovered, promises we haven't yet embraced, and outcomes we haven't yet envisioned. He is the hidden variable in every situation, the trump card yet to be played, the beautiful and satisfying end of the story that looks impossible in the midst of the tortuous, taxing plot. When God is in the mix, no situation is hopeless.

Don't expect disappointment. Don't assume, as so many do, that God will remain distant and not come through in the clutch. Allow your heart to embrace the hope of the whole gospel—not just the Good News of salvation, which is certainly true, but also the good news of His Kingdom, which is coming even now. When God speaks, He is far more interested in filling your heart with expectancy than subduing you with limitations. Embrace the hope that does not disappoint.

Lord, my heart seems so biased toward low expectations. My instinct is to protect myself from disappointment. But Your Kingdom is different; You incline our hearts toward hope. Give me the courage to embrace hope without fear of disappointment. Let me see Your goodness in the land of the living.

DAY 50

I will climb up to my watchtower and stand at my guardpost.

HABAKKUK 2:1

Sometimes people are startled by God's voice. They haven't really been listening for Him, but He steps into their lives anyway with some vital information or direction. That's what He did with Moses, who was hardly looking for a new direction from God when he encountered the burning bush. That's what God did with Samuel, who thought that Eli the priest was calling to him in the middle of the night; he had to be told it was God. And that's what God did with Mary, who may have sought God's will diligently but would never have expected a visit from an angel and an announcement about her beautiful, scandalous pregnancy. God will surprise us when He is about to do something major in His overall plan and wants to use us as part of it. But that isn't the usual way of hearing Him.

No, we will rarely be aware of His voice if we go through life thinking, *If God wants to speak to me, He has my number.* He much more readily speaks to those who are actively listening—who, like Habakkuk, have stationed themselves on the wall and are waiting to hear what God says. This kind of attentiveness requires faith and patience, but eventually it will be rewarded. The more we listen, the more we hear. The more we practice hearing, the more we learn to recognize which voice is God's. Sure, practice involves failure—we will misunderstand some things as we learn—and there will be times when our attentiveness tunes us in to all kinds of voices, not just God's. But over time, we learn to recognize His voice out of all the others.

Whatever it takes, we need to position ourselves like satellite receivers waiting for a signal from the spiritual realm. We need to ask God to speak, and then we need to listen for His voice. He will develop our ears to hear.

Lord, I'm listening. Please speak, and please help me to recognize Your voice. Speak to the questions I've put before You. Give me the pleasure of hearing Your voice clearly.

This foolish plan of God is wiser than the wisest of human plans.

1 CORINTHIANS 1:25

Scripture makes a clear distinction between God's wisdom and our own. In fact, God's wisdom often appears foolish, as Paul points out in referring to the Cross. And human wisdom is often nothing more than foolishness in the eyes of God. Even scriptural wisdom—the maxims in Proverbs that tell us how the world normally works, for example—doesn't apply across the board. What human would have advised Moses to go on an apparent suicide mission into Pharaoh's courts? Or endorsed Hosea's marriage to a prostitute? Or recommended Joshua's circles around Jericho as a viable military strategy? No, God often gives us apparent folly to see if we'll accept it as wisdom, and He often foils the best of our wisdom in order to show Himself wiser.

So when someone advises us to "do what's wise" or to take a live-by-principles approach to life—even when those principles are derived from Scripture—we must insist on the need to hear God's voice, even if He gives us surprising, counterintuitive direction. We may be called fools by many, but the best wisdom comes from hearing God, following Him, and living according to His direction. Eternity will reveal that holy fools were wise and human reasoning was usually foolish. Only those who are willing to embrace God's absurdities—which aren't absurdities at all, from His perspective—are able to enjoy the adventure of a supernatural life.

Deep down inside, we don't crave a relationship with wisdom or with principles. We crave a relationship with God—a personal, living Being who interacts with us daily. Sometimes His voice will seem wise to us, and sometimes it will seem foolish. If we live by our own standards of wisdom, we will receive the former and reject the latter. But all we really need to know is that we have heard. Then we can follow God anywhere—even if it seems absurd.

Father, I trust Your will—even when I don't understand it, and even when others might think I'm foolish for following it. I embrace Your wisdom, no matter how it appears.

The Word became human and made his home among us.

JOHN 1:14

*T*he Gospel of John begins with a startling statement: In the beginning, there was the Word. The Word was with God, but the Word was also God. *With* Him, yet also *Him*. Not another being; the essence of God Himself. We don't understand such mysteries, but that's okay. Finite minds shouldn't be able to understand an infinite being anyway. Still, we wonder. Who is this Word, and why is He called "the Word" in the first place? What would someone known as "the Word" say?

We know from John and the rest of Scripture that the Word is Jesus. He's the wisdom, the *logos* behind creation. When God spoke worlds into being, He spoke through Jesus. Or He spoke Jesus. We aren't sure. However it happened, Jesus was instrumental in creation, and He is one with God. And He is called the Word.

Though that mystery may raise many questions, it also tells us a lot. When Jesus came, He didn't just *speak* the truth. He *was* the truth. And being eternal, He still *is* the truth. That means that when we hear Him, we aren't just receiving words of wisdom or good advice or even eternally significant information. We're receiving *Him*. We can't separate what He *says* from who He *is*. We can't talk about His nature and His voice as if they were two separate entities. Somehow, perhaps mystically, when we receive Jesus by faith and are born of His Spirit, we are born of the Word. Truth is implanted within us. As we grow, we don't just learn His words, we embody them.

Perhaps that's what Jesus meant when He spoke of those who have ears to hear. He wasn't talking about receiving sound waves, but about embodying His nature and His truth. His voice doesn't come to us from outside, but from His Spirit, whom He has put within us. As we embrace the Word, we embody His words.

Lord, You became flesh and lived among us. Enter into my flesh and live through me among Your people. Don't just speak to me; speak through me. Be the Word in me.

Though the LORD is great, he cares for the humble,

but he keeps his distance from the proud.

PSALM 138:6

God is repelled by pride. He keeps His distance from self-sufficient hearts that mistakenly assume they don't need Him. Pride is so contrary to God's nature and so resistant to His ways that He simply stays away. The proud cannot enjoy God's presence and are not sensitive enough to hear His voice. Those who are full of themselves cannot be full of Him.

Humility, on the other hand, draws God closer. He loves the humble-hearted because they know their need for Him and are vulnerable enough to invite Him in. Jesus blessed the poor in spirit because they are empty enough of themselves to have room for God. An unassuming, unpretentious soul is a natural fit for the Spirit of God.

Like worship and gratitude, humility creates the right climate for hearing God. If God keeps His distance from the proud but is drawn to the humble, and if hearing His voice is a by-product of His closeness, then humility is a necessary condition for hearing Him. There are exceptions, of course—the proud

Pharaoh heard God's words through Moses, and the proud King Belshazzar saw the handwriting on the wall. But these were words of warning and judgment, not messages of compassion or calling. When God wants to speak tenderly and lovingly to His people, His voice resonates with clarity in hearts not cluttered with selfishness.

We tend to think of humility as something done to us—an attitude God works in us rather than one we can create—but Scripture tells us to humble *ourselves*. In other words, we are to choose humility over pride, thinking of others before ourselves. When we do, we position ourselves to receive whatever God says.

Lord, if there is anything in me that hinders Your voice—any pride that causes You to withdraw—point it out and help me deal with it. I willingly forsake anything that obstructs my perception of Your will. I gladly empty myself of me in order to be full of You.

[The Lord said,] "Get up and go out into the valley,

and I will speak to you there."

EZEKIEL 3:22

From the Heart of God

"If you want to encounter Me, go where I tell you. Sometimes I whisper to you in the moment, right where you are. Sometimes I meet you in your normal routine. But sometimes you need a change of location. My Son would go to a mountaintop or withdraw from the crowds. Ezekiel had to go to a place where I could show him My glory more fully and privately and then send him back into his normal surroundings. Jeremiah went down to the potter's house so I could give him an illustration. I often put My friends in places that will be relevant to the word I am about to speak, or put them in a strategic spot in order to speak a specific word to them. I have many reasons, and I rarely explain them fully. But when you hear Me telling you to go somewhere, get up and go. When I speak, sometimes location matters.

"I am not bound by geography, but I often use it to make a point.

The topography of the Promised Land is full of subtle messages about My purposes. The paths I led My people on are rich with symbolism. My physical creation and My spiritual truth go hand in hand. If you understand this, you will begin to learn lessons and hear messages in the ways and the places I lead you. I have already filled your life with deep symbolism, and you will begin to notice it. And when you find solitude and privacy, I will unveil Myself more noticeably. Your location can affect what you hear.

"Don't resist the impulses I give you to position yourself to hear. I will make them clear to you, but you must follow them. You will encounter Me in places you never expected."

> Lord, I would go to the ends of the earth to hear Your voice. But I don't want to wander aimlessly. Take me where You want me to go and speak to me there. If You need to change my view to show Your glory, I'm all for it.

DAY 55

It is not you who will be speaking—

it will be the Spirit of your Father speaking through you.

MATTHEW 10:20

*J*esus told His followers that the Spirit would guide them into all truth and tell them about the future (John 16:13). Paul assured his readers often that Jesus lived in them—willing, working, and speaking the things of God. Peter told his readers to speak as if they were speaking the very words of God (1 Peter 4:11). In Matthew 10, Jesus gives His followers a glimpse of what that will look like. There are times when they will speak—with their voices, their thoughts, and seemingly their words—but it will actually be the Spirit speaking through them. They will be the speakers, but God will be the source.

Few people today are apt to claim divine inspiration when they speak, but that comes more from humility than from biblical conviction. It also comes from a lack of faith in what God has promised, as well as too much sensitivity to pharisaical critics. Often when someone in the church today claims to have heard from God—or more daringly, to have spoken His words—hypervigilant "defenders of the faith" will declare such audacity to be practically heretical. But these kinds of critics, in defending the Bible, have forgotten what the Bible actually says. They have ignored the words of Jesus or redefined them to apply only to one generation of disciples or apostles. Meanwhile, those who have heard God's voice are intimidated into thinking they haven't.

Jesus was emphatic that the Spirit speaks through His followers with the Father's own words. It isn't heretical to believe that truth. In fact, *not* believing it falls far short of God's purposes. Instead, we are invited to let the Spirit rise up within us and speak boldly through our mouths in the situations around us— not arrogantly, not presumptuously, but confidently. The Spirit loves to make Himself heard through His people.

Holy Spirit, I know You are speaking, and I trust that You are speaking to me and through me. You give me permission to declare what I've heard from You to others. Help me make the most of every opportunity to do so.

DAY 56

The LORD asked [Moses], "What is that in your hand?"

EXODUS 4:2

*M*oses raised all kinds of objections to God's call—
apparently a burning bush wasn't convincing in itself—so God
had to prove that His power would accompany Moses back to
Egypt. God could have sent Moses to find a special rod with
magical powers from a secret hiding place in the wilderness,
but there was no need for such theatrics. The rod itself wasn't
the issue; God could demonstrate His power in the rod Moses
already had. So when He told Moses to throw down the rod and
it became a serpent—and then a rod again when Moses picked it
back up—the symbolism was profound. God's power accompa-
nies what we already have in our hands if we use it according to
His direction.

Your life is filled with assets: your natural gifts and talents,
spiritual gifts, material resources, education and experience, job,
geographic location, and more. These aren't a random collection
of memories or coincidences. They are collateral for the work of
God's Kingdom. That means you can often discern God's voice
from what He has already put into your hands. Whether it's

possessions, positions, or knowledge and experience, you have things that God has probably long intended to use. His voice will likely tell you to throw it down before Him and see what He does with it.

That doesn't mean God always aims for the status quo in your life. In fact, He rarely does. But He also tends to build on what He has already given you. Whatever you hear from Him as you seek direction, it will probably include some things that are already in your hand. As you "throw them down"—offer them to Him for His use—some of them will come alive in ways you've never experienced before. What He has done in your past very often points toward what He will do in your future.

> *Lord, the past You have guided me through is speaking to me about the future You are guiding me into. Show me what You can do with the things in my hands. All I have is Yours to use.*

DAY 57

I [Paul] pray that from his glorious, unlimited resources he will

empower you with inner strength through his Spirit.

EPHESIANS 3:16

*T*he visiting speaker had a reputation for insightful prophetic words—expressing God's heart for people in situations that no stranger could have known on his own. And even during this service, he spoke directly into the lives of people with remarkable precision.

A woman who had come with a desperate plea for God to give her specific confirmation about her calling had high expectations. And those expectations were dashed when the speaker finally called her out and simply said, "Trust God."

That wasn't the specific word she was looking for, and she was deeply disappointed. But she went back to the next service with high hopes again. And when she heard the same message to "trust God," she was crushed. Why wouldn't God give her specific confirmation like He was doing for so many around her? Why would He remain silent on matters He had clearly spoken to her about before? After praying through her confusion and pain, she realized the answer. She had already heard

God clearly; asking for another confirmation came from a lack of trust. God was letting her know she could rely on what she had already heard.

Can you trust the Holy Spirit who is in you? That's what many of our questions about His will come down to. We can be so worried about being mistaken that we forget His greater power to keep us in the truth. We're suspicious of anything in our own hearts, even when we've received direct promises and confirmation about God's work in us and His will for our lives. We forget that Jesus is in us and we can trust His Spirit. What He has spoken within our hearts is just as valid as what He speaks to us through others. When He is silent outwardly, we can rest in what He says inwardly.

> *Holy Spirit, may I never be guilty of downplaying the treasure You've put in me. You are completely trustworthy, and You reside within me. Inspire me with Your desires and direction, and give me the faith to believe.*

DAY 58

I had not told anyone about the plans God had put in my heart for Jerusalem.

NEHEMIAH 2:12

$\mathcal{T}$he woman had been noticing a trend, and her heart was burdened by it. Single parents from an economically challenged neighborhood would drop their children off at church on Sunday mornings and leave. Some in the congregation were offended—"The church isn't a babysitting service," they would say—but she saw it as an opportunity. The kids needed God, and by investing attention in them in Sunday school, the church would also have an avenue into the lives of the parents. This was not an intrusion; it was an open invitation from the Father.

The woman asked the pastor whether the church could expand their Sunday school to meet the specific needs of the children and their families. Wisely, he deferred action back to the one who had the vision for it. "Sure, we can help them. Why don't you develop a plan for it?" At first intimidated, then inspired, she grabbed hold of the vision and ran with it. God had put the burden in her heart for a reason. She was the one He was calling to intervene.

As Nehemiah affirmed before moving to Jerusalem, God

puts His purposes into the hearts of His people. He gives a sense of mission and calling to those who can take the lead in meeting the needs around them. We may think our burdens are for others to fulfill, and others may certainly be involved. But our burdens are usually the prompting of the Holy Spirit—not for someone else to do something about the problem, but for us to address it ourselves. Where there's a strong vision to fulfill a Kingdom-oriented purpose, the Spirit has been speaking. And no matter how intimidated we may feel, we're to begin walking in that direction and follow as the Spirit leads.

> *Holy Spirit, help me sort out the burdens in my heart. Are they all Yours? Which ones should I follow? Lead me to fulfill the purposes You have placed within me. Clarify my vision and secure my steps. Lead me through open doors to accomplish Your Kingdom mission wherever I can.*

DAY 59

His Spirit searches out everything and shows us God's deep secrets.

1 CORINTHIANS 2:10

*G*od knows all things. As Creator of the universe, He knows even the deepest mysteries it contains. He knows every "why" and "how" of existence, the answers to all those questions that nag us about our purpose and destiny. His Spirit knows every motive of the Father's heart and every nuance of His relationship with us. He is a guardian of deep secrets.

In Christ, many of those deep secrets are unveiled—Paul wrote often of the "mystery" of the gospel that was being revealed in his generation. Yet Scripture implies that there are more secrets to be known, and logic confirms it. An infinite God must always know more than He has revealed and always harbor thoughts that finite minds cannot fathom. We don't know exactly how history will unfold, for example, though God has revealed its general direction and ultimate goal. We don't know exactly how our lives will unfold either, though God has given us a purpose and continues to call us forward. There are Scripture passages that we have not yet fully grasped, reasons behind evil and suffering that we can't even remotely understand, dynamics of human relationships that we haven't sorted out yet. Although God has unveiled many secrets, the details are often still hidden.

But God's Spirit shows us His deep secrets. The wisdom of the world can never grasp the heart and mind of God, but He shares His counsel with those who love Him. He wants to reveal His nature and His plans to those whose hearts belong to Him. He doesn't tell us to figure things out or to rely on our own wisdom; He invites us into His private counsel. When we are immersed in His Spirit, we begin to understand things we never understood before. We have sudden ideas that we know are not our own. And we begin to walk in directions we had never planned on. Why? Because the deep secrets of God are unfolding in our hearts.

> *Holy Spirit, work Your secrets into my heart. Every day,*
> *show me more of You.*

DAY 60

We all, who with unveiled faces contemplate the Lord's glory,

are being transformed into his image with ever-increasing glory,

which comes from the Lord, who is the Spirit.

2 CORINTHIANS 3:18, NIV

*A*m I in tune with God's Spirit? Am I exercising His gifts appropriately? Are my desires in line with His? Am I praying according to His will? Am I hearing His voice? If we can't answer these questions with a high degree of certainty, we will walk out our relationship with God tentatively. We will make decisions, offer prayers, and listen for His guidance without much conviction, and our uncertain faith will waver. There's a lot of humility in this walk, but not a lot of holy boldness. And we can't accomplish much in God's Kingdom without both.

The most significant variable in answering these questions is whether we are gazing at Jesus or not. When He is front and center in our minds and hearts—when He is bigger and better than our deepest desires, getting our prayers answered, and discovering God's will—He will align us with His heartbeat. When we contemplate His glory and pursue Him above all else, we are transformed into His image without even being aware of it. We become like whatever we love, so if Christ is our greatest love—not just in theory, but in daily consciousness—we become like Him. And as we do, we hear, pray, walk, and talk like He does. Just as He is the radiance of the Father, we reflect God's radiance too. We don't have to worry about being misguided when our greatest passion is knowing Jesus.

When Jesus becomes and remains the focus of our attention, a lot of other things in life fall into place and a lot of spiritual questions get resolved. We may not know exactly how that happens, but it does. Our perspective changes. Even our questions change. And uncertainties about our relationship with God begin to vanish.

> *Jesus, may my gaze never depart from You. Show me Your glory. Impart Your nature to me. Implant Your heartbeat within me. Be my truest and deepest passion.*

DAY 61

I was in the Spirit on the Lord's Day, and I heard . . .

REVELATION 1:10, NKJV

*W*hat did John mean by being "in the Spirit on the Lord's Day"? Was he talking about a particular day of the week? Probably not—the phrase "the Lord's Day," or "the day of the Lord," is almost always used in Scripture to refer to judgment and is never used to refer to a Sabbath. And what does he mean by being "in the Spirit"? Is he in a vision or a trance leading up to the time that he sees heaven opened? Or is he simply in sync and in deep fellowship with the Spirit? Regardless of these details, we can draw some pretty clear conclusions: John was in some kind of deep devotional or worshipful frame of mind when he heard the Lord speak.

Does that mean we always need to be in some meditative state to hear God's voice? Of course not. After all, there are some rather exceptional aspects to the visions of Revelation; it's not exactly a pattern to follow. It does, however, point to a dynamic that occurs often in Scripture. A well-cultivated, meaningful, worshipful relationship with God creates an environment in which we are much more likely to hear Him speak.

He sometimes comes upon the unsuspecting—Moses and Paul are notable examples—but He more often draws near to those who have come near to Him. Just as we recognize the voices of those with whom we spend the most time, so will we recognize God's voice as we spend ample time with Him. What begins as a whisper grows into a shout if we are in close fellowship with the Holy Spirit.

That ought to motivate us to draw closer in worship, in prayer, and even in just resting in His presence. Time is never better spent than when we spend it in fellowship with God's Spirit. That's where relationships deepen, and deep relationships are where He loves to speak.

Holy Spirit, I offer myself to You—to be "in" You, on any day, and to hear whatever You want to say. Draw me into the closeness of relationship that causes You to want to share Your heart.

DAY 62

[Jesus said,] "Look, I have given you authority over all the power of the enemy,

and you can walk among snakes and scorpions and crush them."

LUKE 10:19

*O*ur hearts are hungry for truth—so hungry, in fact, that we must be careful not to consume lies. Our ears are open to God, but they also hear other messages. We perceive words and thoughts that produce fear, discouragement, depression, confusion, doubt, and all sorts of other destructive emotions and attitudes. Those are deceptive enough, but there are subtler counterfeits than that—messages that promise what God hasn't promised, that offer us what's good instead of what's best, or that pledge to fulfill God-ordained dreams in corrupt ways. God speaks exclusive truths into our lives, yet the contradictions are almost limitless.

A necessary aspect of hearing truth is refusing to hear lies. To accept God's voice is to reject others. We don't have to be victims of false messages. God has given us authority over the deceptions of the enemy and even the deceptions of our own hearts. When we refuse to fuel them with our own biases and inclinations and become merciless toward any thought that isn't captive to

Christ, the deceptions begin to crumble and the truth doesn't. Discernment is much easier when truth is the last word standing.

Pray for discernment with authority. Don't be tentative. From the moment God puts His spotlight on a counterfeit message, refuse to entertain it. Take every thought captive to Christ, pulling down philosophies and agendas, and even subtle attitudes that don't fit His character or His purposes. Trample on any hint of guidance that conflicts with what God has already revealed. Relentlessly pursue the dreams and calling He has put within you. If they are His dreams, they must be accomplished His way. Any tempting words that are inconsistent with His voice are worthy of being crushed.

> *Lord, if You give me the discernment to recognize counterfeits, I will be ruthless with them. False messages will not take root in my heart. Establish in me only Your words, and let me live them without compromise.*

DAY 63

Your salvation will come like the dawn, and your wounds

will quickly heal. Your godliness will lead you forward,

and the glory of the LORD will protect you from behind.

ISAIAH 58:8

From the Heart of God

"You've waited for resolution to the problems in your life and for the fulfillment of your deep longings. You've sought My will on these matters, and I've given you some direction on them. But your focus on the things that pertain to you has blinded you to some of the other things I've been saying. If you will widen the range of your hearing—and follow the instructions that don't apply specifically to what you're focusing on right now—the solutions and fulfillments will come. When you learn the art of focusing your prayers and activities on other people's needs rather than your own, you'll look back and discover that I'm giving unusual help to the things that concern you. Getting your attention off of your needs draws My attention to them.

"Sometimes you look to Me for answers while I'm looking back at you for answers. Both of us are asking, 'Why don't you do something?' When you respond to what I've told you, I'll respond to what you've asked Me. That doesn't mean I'm waiting for your perfection, of course. I'm waiting for the leaning of your heart to change. Turn your steps in the right direction and I'll quicken your steps and come running toward you.

"This is one of the hardest practices for you to develop, but it's one that prompts Me to bring your salvation like the dawn. Like a watchman waiting for the morning, you've looked for My help. I can assure you that help will come, but not because you're obsessing about your longings. It's because you've paid attention to Mine. I will demonstrate My power toward those who demonstrate their love for Me."

> *Lord, I desperately long for my salvation to come like the dawn. I have gaping wounds and screaming needs that demand to be healed and resolved. Give me a heart for the world at large, but please rebuild my small corner of it.*

[The Lord] said to me, "Prophesy to these bones and say to them,

'Dry bones, hear the word of the LORD!'"

EZEKIEL 37:4, NIV

God showed Ezekiel a vision of a valley full of bones. Not the bones of the recently deceased, but dry bones. In other words, these bones were far removed from any hint of life. Yet God tells Ezekiel to prophesy to the bones to command them to hear God's word. The prophet speaks life and breath into them.

Why would the living God need a human to command bones to hear His voice? Can't God make His voice heard to anyone or anything He wants? Of course He can, but He is demonstrating a lesson in this vision. God implements His will through partnership with His people. He rarely does anything in human affairs without prompting a human spokesperson to pray for it or speak it. Apparently, God takes seriously the commission He gives in Genesis—the assignment for humanity to govern the earth. And apparently, there's something to Amos's comment that God does nothing without telling His prophets (Amos 3:7). When God wants to intervene on earth,

He partners with someone who will hear His words, respond to them, and speak them.

We don't fully understand the role we have in declaring God's will, but we know we're called to do it. Our words have power; God's universe is wired that way. What we say has a practical and spiritual effect on the course of events. Our words shape our lives, the lives of people around us, and the environment we live in. And when our words line up with what God has spoken to us, we can change the course of history. His will is accomplished through them. Even dry bones come to life at the sound of a human voice in tune with God.

Lord, tell me what to say. Inspire my words and give life to the things I declare. Whenever You prompt me, I will speak life into dead situations, truth into deceptive circumstances, and possibility into impossibilities—and then watch Your Spirit work. May my voice line up with Yours and accomplish great things for Your Kingdom.

Once again David asked God what to do. "Do not attack them

straight on," God replied. "Instead, circle around behind

and attack them near the poplar trees."

1 CHRONICLES 14:14

*D*avid had just won a victory over the Philistines by getting permission and direction from God. So when the Philistines attacked again, David could have simply assumed God's previous guidance still applied. But David was wise enough to know that God's direction varies from time to time and situation to situation, so he asked again. This time, God directed him quite specifically to take a different tack. Yesterday's instructions did not suffice for today.

We need to live by that truth. God's nature never changes, so any instructions He gives us based on His character will always apply. But His methods often change, so we need to ask Him repeatedly for specific direction. He won one battle by having His people march around a city, won another by reducing an army to three hundred men, and won this one by signaling His people with the sound of feet marching in the trees. All these approaches were one-time strategies, never repeated in biblical history, even in similar situations. God refuses to let us live exclusively by principles. We must stay in close relationship with Him, keeping our ears open, in order to know what to do.

Whatever you are facing today, listen to God for the right approach. Yesterday's methods may or may not be God's desire for you today. You are in unique circumstances, and you need unique guidance. Precepts and principles aren't enough; like daily bread that needs to be eaten fresh each day, the voice of God is your nourishment. Ask Him for a fresh word, listening for His guidance every step of the way. He will speak specifically to your need.

> *Lord, what should I do? I don't have enough wisdom for the demands of this day, but You do, so my eyes are on You. I desperately need Your guidance. Please make it clear.*

I posted watchmen over you who said, "Listen for the sound of the alarm."

But you replied, "No! We won't pay attention!"

JEREMIAH 6:17

Both God and Jeremiah were frustrated. Jeremiah lamented that no one listened when he spoke (Jeremiah 6:10). His message wasn't popular. Now God affirms Jeremiah's lament. Although He had posted watchmen (prophets) among His people, the people had shut their ears and determined not to pay attention. They were open only to certain messages, things they wanted to hear that turned out to be false. They missed God's voice because they tuned it out.

The number one obstacle to hearing God is a calloused heart. Those who ask, seek, and knock will receive, find, and walk through open doors; but we live in a world full of people who set their own agendas and are not asking to hear from God. Even God's own people had shut Him out in Jeremiah's time— as well as in many other eras of history—and did not want to hear. They ignored warnings, listened to flattery, and clung to their own agendas. They chose spiritual deafness.

Always approach God with a willingness to hear the exact

opposite of what you want to hear. You don't have to approach Him with that expectation; He is usually much more encouraging than that. But there's a vast difference between expectation and openness, and though we expect affirmation from Him, we need to be open to hear correction or direction that goes against our surface desires. Listening to God selectively tends to cultivate spiritual deafness; when we refuse to hear in one area, we limit our hearing in other areas too. But when we open ourselves to anything God wants to say, He can say anything. When He has our attention, He is much more generous with His.

Lord, there are things I don't want You to say to me—things that don't fit with my dreams and desires—yet if they are Your will, I need to hear them. My ears are open even to Your correction. I am paying full attention to You.

The word of God is alive and powerful.

HEBREWS 4:12

God breathed His words through human beings. That's what *inspired* means: "breathed into." The Bible is a mysterious mix of the divine and human, with the divine guiding the thoughts and expressions of humans who encountered Him and spoke and wrote what they experienced and learned. When the Word was written, it was under the specific guidance and supervision of the Holy Spirit.

The Word is also inspired when it is read and heard today. The Spirit's activity didn't end once the words were on ancient scrolls. He is working even now, causing specific messages to jump off the page into our hearts, provoking our minds to encounter truth and wrestle with it, encouraging our hearts to believe and grow, and imparting truth and wisdom into our spirits. Yes, it's possible to read Scripture purely from the mind, with human thoughts and skepticism and motives filtering the words to the point that they have little power. But when our spirits are open, the voice in the Word comes alive. Scripture still speaks.

We often strain to hear God's voice while our Bibles lie

smoldering on the shelf, waiting to breathe God's words into us. And though He speaks through a multitude of messengers, we hear best when Scripture is an integral part of our hearing process. The Word is the necessary context for all other hearing. When we forget that, we're likely to get skewed messages from spurious sources. But when we feed on the Bible—which is still very much alive and powerful—the voice of God simmers and stirs within us. He fills us with truth.

Don't just read the Bible. Saturate yourself with it. Savor it. Let it shape your heart, your mind, and your spirit. When you do, it will open your ears.

Holy Spirit, breathe Your words into me. Don't just teach me Your truth; fill me with it. Let it shape me in every way so I can hear Your voice in it, through it, and by the light of it.

DAY 68

For the sake of your name lead and guide me.

PSALM 31:3, NIV

*T*he pastor had sensed a transition was coming to his church. He just didn't know the transition would come about because of his departure. He had no intention of leaving until God began to raise the question in his heart. He asked if he was hearing correctly, but he could hardly believe the direction. Then a friend in another city texted him to say he sensed God was about to move him. And when he traveled to another country for a speaking engagement, the host pastor said, "I see God giving you an exit ramp that you need to take." Another leader in the next city gave essentially the same message. None of these people had heard from each other or from the pastor about this time of transition. They had simply sensed it from God's Spirit. The convergence of the message confirmed the surprising word God had been speaking.

God doesn't typically use the words of other people to inform us of a new direction, but He very often speaks through others to confirm something we've already been praying about. In fact, He sometimes lets us quietly wrestle with a decision until we come to grips with it and choose, and only then will He confirm what we've already arrived at by faith. He doesn't take away the need for faith up front; He lets us flex our faith muscles until He's ready to support us with His affirmation. It's rarely a smooth process, but it's an effective one. He guides us with skillful hands even when we think we're wandering.

Be very cautious when someone says that God has given him or her a message for you that would require a significant change of direction. But if you think God has already been leading you in a new direction and still aren't sure, don't be surprised if He uses the words of others to confirm it. He knows how to guide, and He lets others be part of the process.

Lord, I listen earnestly for Your guidance, but You never told me to listen alone. Give me timely words from others—and discernment to know when to heed them.

DAY 69

[The Lord said,] "In those days when you pray, I will listen.

If you look for me wholeheartedly, you will find me."

Charles Finney was in a wrestling match with his own soul to give his heart to God. He resolved one Sunday in 1821 to settle the question of his salvation once and for all, before all other concerns in his life, and he spent days trying to pray and grasp the truth of the gospel. The next Wednesday, on his way to the office, he heard an inward voice: *What are you **waiting** for? Are you endeavoring to earn a righteousness of your own?* Immediately, he saw the fullness of the atonement of Christ. And later, while on his knees before God, yet worried that someone might see him, a passage of Scripture "seemed to drop" into his mind—the promise of Jeremiah 29:13 that those who seek God wholeheartedly will find Him. Finney had vowed to give his heart to God, and the verse assured him that his vow could be fulfilled and his gift would be accepted. He suddenly saw his faith as a matter of the will and not of the intellect. Over the next few days, he experienced the presence of Jesus and the love of God in profoundly personal ways.

God has promised that He will speak to us, especially to our searching hearts. Once Finney determined to settle the question of his salvation, he heard an inward voice, sensed God's leading, and experienced relevant verses coming to mind in the moment he needed them. There was no need to question whether he was hearing God; God was leading him into salvation and a life of fruitful ministry. Finney simply followed what the Spirit was doing in him, acutely aware of the burdens of sin, and yet also aware of the freedom in Christ that was offered to him. He heard God because he desperately sought Him. God makes the same promise to every soul who wrestles with the questions of His truth and is willing to follow the sound of His voice.

Lord, may my heart follow the burdens, the convictions, the joys, the freedoms, and the insights You give me—in full confidence that You are speaking to me.

[Jesus said,] "I have given them the glory you gave me, so they may be one as we are one. I am in them and you are in me. May they experience such perfect unity that the world will know that you sent me."

JOHN 17:22-23

Normally, Jesus' prayer for oneness is seen as a call for Christian unity. When He says, "So they may be one," we instinctively add the words "with each other." It certainly includes that, but it's more. We can just as easily add the words "with Me" and understand this as a prayer for oneness with God Himself. After all, the rest of the sentence implies something far more supernatural and mystical than we're accustomed to. Jesus is praying that we may be one with Him in the very same way that He is one with the Father.

How is Jesus *one* with the Father? In motives, in desires, in mission and purpose, in character and attributes, and even in substance. He has already made that clear in His teachings: "The Father and I are one," He said to an infuriated crowd (John 10:30). Now He prays for that kind of oneness with *us*. It's an invitation into the fellowship of the Trinity. We are united at our very core with the life of God Himself.

When Ezekiel and Jeremiah prophesy a new heart, and Acts

describes the coming of the Spirit, and Paul says that it's God working within us, the picture we get is far more than a new set of motives and desires. It's an inner union between us and the substance of God. The practical aspects of this union aren't inevitable—many Christians live in rebellion or apathy—but they are certainly available. We can truly know that He is powerfully dwelling in us and that His life within us has very practical implications. One of those implications is that the Word Himself speaks. Within. Almost constantly. And we can hear because this is why He came.

> *Jesus, fulfill this union in every way possible. Let me have Your heartbeat and breathe Your breath. And may Your voice flow through me and out of me constantly.*

Jesus answered his thoughts. "Simon," he said to the Pharisee,

"I have something to say to you."

LUKE 7:40

Simon the Pharisee observed a sinful woman intruding on his dinner party and tried to make a point about her. He needed a new perspective, so Jesus gave him one—through a story. Jesus could have simply rebuked him or started an argument with this stuck-in-his-ways religious leader; a direct confrontation would have provoked an entertaining and heated discussion. But it would have been a fruitless one. What was the way into Simon's heart? A metaphor. An illustration. A story that the man could relate to.

With this illustration, Jesus made the point that Simon had been looking at this woman through the wrong lenses. As most experts in the law tended to do, Simon's biggest issue in such situations was how to establish separation between righteousness and sinfulness and, more specifically, how to remain unstained by sin and take a stand against it. Jesus showed him the relationship behind the event. The woman wasn't there to corrupt the guests; she was there to express deep gratitude to the Savior who had cleansed her. Her love for Jesus was entirely appropriate. Simon's attitude toward her wasn't.

This is often how God speaks to us—through stories, metaphors, illustrations, and visual case studies. The circumstances in our lives are frequently much more than just circumstances; they are object lessons in what God wants us to learn. He speaks through them, just as He spoke to Simon. Why? Because this is the language that can pierce the barriers of our hearts. We can understand illustrations. They can give us a radically new perspective—*if* we know to look for a new perspective in them.

Notice what God is saying through the stories around you. Is He making a point? Shedding different light on an old problem? Reshaping your sympathies and expectations? Very often, He is. His voice can be challenging. But if we accept His challenges, they can change our lives.

Jesus, feel free to challenge me like You challenged Simon. I'm open to change. I invite You to reshape my perspective, even if it stretches me out of my comfort zone.

[The Lord said,] "When I give you a message,

I will loosen your tongue and let you speak."

EZEKIEL 3:27

From the Heart of God

"My Son told His followers not to worry about what they would say in crucial moments. My Spirit would give them the words. That has always been true of those who are close to My heart, and it always will be. Like the prophets and the disciples, you will find yourself in strategic circumstances and realize words are flowing easily. They will sound like your words because they are coming out of your mouth, but they will be words I have given you. When you need to express My truth, I will loosen your tongue to speak it.

"Don't be surprised that your personality and Mine are growing closer together. Don't be alarmed if you have difficulty figuring out which thoughts are yours and which are Mine. You don't always have to know the difference. Ask for discernment, but expect Me to fill your heart and mind with Myself. You've asked that your mind would be renewed, your character would be conformed to the image of Christ, and your actions would be consistent with Mine. Why wouldn't your speech be transformed too? I will use you as My mouthpiece and fill you with My truth.

"For this to happen, you will need to cooperate with the process. Ask Me to fill your mouth with My words and then expect Me to do so. Rest in faith and trust that I am working within you to express My voice. You won't become infallible, but you will be inspired. Believe that I will give you messages to share with those around you. They will feel the weight of My words even when they don't recognize My voice. And you will experience the power of My purposes and the joy of being My messenger."

> Lord, use my words to impact others. Loosen my tongue to express Your messages. May I never dismiss my words as insignificant. They always have the potential to reveal Your heart.

[The Lord said,] "I am watching to see that my word is fulfilled."

JEREMIAH 1:12, NIV

*C*ountless people are holding on to what they believe is a God-given dream, vision, or purpose—and are thoroughly frustrated by how long it's taking to happen or how many detours they have had to take. It can be extremely painful to live between a promise and its fulfillment, wondering whether it has been lost, forgotten, forfeited, thwarted, or eternally delayed. It often seems as if God speaks and then sits on His words without doing anything about them.

As frustrating as this is, it's normal for God. He gave Joseph dreams and then took long years and a very winding path to make them manifest. He anointed David as king and then let obstacles to his throne stand in the way for a confusingly extended time. Abraham, Moses, Caleb and Joshua, the captives of Babylon—all of them waited far longer than they expected to. God has a confounding tendency to speak long before He plans to fulfill.

Even while we wait, God is working behind the scenes. And during the process, our faith is stretched seemingly beyond its breaking point, though in the end, we find that it hasn't broken. We wrestle with God, ask many questions, cry out in desperation, and exercise more spiritual muscles than we thought we had. And it's terribly uncomfortable. But it's necessary. This is how God develops His people and prepares them for the weight of their calling.

Don't give up on the things God has spoken. It may seem that He has forgotten them or chosen another direction, but He hasn't. He had enough foresight to speak only what He intended to accomplish. If He has said it, He will act on it. He is watching to see that His words are fulfilled.

Lord, I don't understand why Your process takes so long, nor why the path is so indirect. But I trust You. I know Your words are true, even years after You've spoken them. I'm choosing to cling to them in faith.

You must not turn away from any of the commands I am giving you today,

nor follow after other gods and worship them.

DEUTERONOMY 28:14

*M*any religions seek to shape behavior. They emphasize the outward result. In our relationship with God, motives
matter—even more than our outward actions do. It's true that
much of Scripture gives instructions about what to do, but never
apart from the context of our loving God and being loved by
Him. The relationship, not the behavior, is the priority. All of
our actions should flow out of that relationship.

In Deuteronomy, God's people are told repeatedly to stay
close to God's commands and refuse to turn away from them.
But some verses don't leave it at that; they give us glimpses
into God's deeper desire. He isn't seeking a people who will
simply follow orders. He's seeking people who will love Him
and respond to Him by becoming like Him in nature. Both
obedience and disobedience are matters of the heart, not of
self-discipline. Again and again, heeding His instructions is
juxtaposed with the alternative of following after other gods and
worshiping them. We don't just follow His words; we follow

Him. We aren't just committed; we give Him our love. He isn't just our God; He's our *only* God. This is the only context in which hearing God's voice will be fruitful or satisfying. Anything less is just stale religion.

That's why it's vital to respond with diligence to the words God has spoken. It's all about relationship and His jealous desire for our love. There are consequences—it's no accident that instructions like these are emphasized in Deuteronomy 28–29, where the blessings of obedience and curses of disobedience are graphically laid out—so it's in our best interests to listen closely. But our deeper motive is to love God with all our hearts. With God, motives always matter.

> *Father, I do love You; help me love You more. Following Your words works out well for me, but may I always do it to please You. May my heart always be motivated by passion for You.*

DAY 75

[The serpent] asked the woman, "Did God really say . . . ?"

GENESIS 3:1

*L*ord, teach me something about You that I don't already know."
As is sometimes the case, God's answer came through an unpleas-
ant circumstance. I was being misrepresented by a slanderer, and
even some people who once respected me were starting to get a
false impression. I was outraged, of course; most of us become
offended when our pride is wounded for any reason, especially a
false one. I did not respond well. But there was nothing I could
do to stop the smears. All I could do was continue to be myself
and trust that people who knew me well would know the truth.

During this painful season, I was hit with a disturbing
thought: *God is misrepresented millions of times every day.* Even
people who should know Him and love Him well are sometimes
swayed by the lies. The Accuser whispers slanderous thoughts
against God almost constantly. The One whose love is higher,
longer, deeper, and wider than we can imagine has His love questioned all the time by millions who think He doesn't care or isn't
there. The world lives in suspicion of God's goodness because a
con artist has misrepresented Him for thousands of years.

This must grieve God's heart deeply. He created us to know Him and love Him and to pour His love into others. Yet His relationship with us encounters constant interference; and unless we relentlessly cling to what we know to be true, the interference is effective. We spend much of our lives in a battle to trust God's goodness. But if we saw clearly, trust would never be an issue.

God shows us the truth in the words of Scripture, so we already know. But the message sinks into our hearts much deeper when He gives us a taste of what He experiences. He moves our hearts to understand how His heart is moved.

Lord, I invite You to move my heart anytime to synchronize it with Yours. I need to connect with You. Only Your voice, Your expressions, Your revelation can accomplish that. Give me insights into who You are.

DAY 76

[Jesus said,] "The hearts of these people are hardened, and their ears cannot

hear, and they have closed their eyes—so their eyes cannot see,

and their ears cannot hear, and their hearts cannot understand,

and they cannot turn to me and let me heal them."

MATTHEW 13:15

A hardened heart is the enemy of God's voice and a frightening spiritual danger. God is perfectly willing to correct a mistaken heart, give wisdom to a simple heart, sway a reluctant heart, and awaken a sleeping heart. But a hardened heart requires softening, and that usually takes time. God doesn't force His way into the spirit of a calloused soul. He woos and pursues, often very persuasively and even irresistibly, but He doesn't demand. He is looking for a loving response, not an obligatory one. Hearts that have grown cold and calloused effectively keep Him out, and He lets them.

That hardening isn't always a conscious choice. In fact, it usually isn't. Little by little, we may desensitize ourselves to whatever God is doing in our lives, slowly and imperceptibly growing cold to His overtures. We justify and rationalize and come up with lots of explanations—many of which may even sound spiritual—for relying on our own wisdom and making our own decisions, but they all create distance between us and God. Over time, our hearts harden and our ears forget how to hear. We become spiritually dull.

Whatever it takes, develop your sensitivity to God and His whispers in your life. Ask Him to tune you in to the sound of His voice. Don't wait for Him to shake the foundations of your life to get your attention. Give Him your full attention every day. Devour Scripture, watch for His words, and look for ways to apply them. Let the softening of your heart draw you into God's nourishing, healing, strengthening presence.

Lord, is my heart calloused? Have I tuned You out? It's difficult to recognize hardness in myself, and I need to know. In any areas of insensitivity in my life, soften me up. Draw me close. Get my attention and hold it. Heighten my spiritual senses to pick up on even the slightest whisper from You.

The rain and snow come down from the heavens and stay on the ground to water the earth. They cause the grain to grow, producing seed for the farmer and bread for the hungry. It is the same with my word. I send it out, and it always produces fruit. It will accomplish all I want it to, and it will prosper everywhere I send it.

ISAIAH 55:10-11

Some of us speak with little expectation of our words being heeded. Parents give instructions, sometimes repeatedly, knowing that their children may forget them or choose to ignore them. People speak of their future dreams without much confidence that they will come to pass. Counselors give advice, realizing that their advice will only sometimes be followed. To many of us, words are just words.

The result is a culture of language in which "all talk and no action" is a frequent lament. We tell people to put their money where their mouth is and describe their inaction and empty promises as "only words." But with God, there is no "only" about words. His words are as good as done. Like seeds sown into fertile ground, they will yield a harvest. When He issues an order, it will be carried out. When He gives a promise, it will be fulfilled. When He declares His purposes, they will be accomplished. As some versions of this passage say, God's Word will not return to Him empty. It will result in what He wants it to do.

Understand that when we hear God's voice, it's a weighty matter. He isn't just suggesting an option; He's declaring His truth. We can't afford to listen to Him simply out of curiosity. We must listen with a sacred resolve to align with His words. If they are instructions, we will carry them out. If they are promises, we will believe them. If they are encouragement or correction, we will accept it. Whatever He says, it's true. It will not return to Him without fulfilling His purpose.

Lord, if all creation heeds Your voice, so must I. Let the distance between my ears and my actions be short. I respond with yes to whatever You say.

[Moses said to God,] "If it is true that you look favorably on me,

let me know your ways so I may understand you more fully

and continue to enjoy your favor."

EXODUS 33:13

*I*f it is true . . ." Our theological conscience might cringe over that lead-in, as it seems to question God's word. After all, God had already made His favor clear to Moses. He had chosen Moses, called him, used him to lead the Israelites out of Egypt, delivered him miraculously from the ire of impatient Israelites and a vengeful Pharaoh, and given him unprecedented revelation at the top of Mount Sinai. God's favor on Moses was clearly unquestionable. Yet Moses questioned it.

Apparently, despite all the revelation God had given him, Moses didn't sense that he knew enough about God's ways to continue to please Him. He had seen mixtures of God's power, His love, and His anger, and Moses was still trying to comprehend the strange events of recent history. God had already spoken with him face-to-face, already guided him through all sorts of challenges, and already revealed quite a few laws and expectations for His covenant people. Yet the heart of this God remained elusive.

We can know for certain that we'll never arrive at a place of knowing all there is to know about God. We will always be able to go deeper, to see new facets of His nature and expect the unexpected. We'll never fully get a handle on who He is. But we can *trust* who He is and know that He will be reliable. When we explore His nature, we will get to know Him better. But we will never be able to define Him.

That's why Moses' prayer doesn't callously disregard what God has already done for him. No matter how much we've seen and heard, we are right to ask to see and hear more. And as He did with Moses, God will honor that request with an answer.

Lord, if it's true that You look favorably on me—and You've made it clear through Your Son that You do—show me more. Lead me on an adventure of knowing You more fully every day.

DAY 79

An angel of the Lord said to [Philip], "Go south down the desert road. . . ."

So he started out, and he met the treasurer of Ethiopia. . . . The Holy Spirit

said to Philip, "Go over and walk along beside the carriage." Philip ran over

and heard the man reading from the prophet Isaiah. . . . Beginning with this

same Scripture, Philip told him the Good News about Jesus.

ACTS 8:26-27, 29-30, 35

*P*hilip was carrying out a fruitful ministry in Samaria when an angel gave him instructions to go to a remote desert road along the Mediterranean in Gaza. While Philip was there, the Holy Spirit spoke to him about an Ethiopian traveler he encountered. The Ethiopian was reading Scripture. And then Philip spoke God's message to him. Here in the space of a few short verses, we can observe several modes of God's voice, and we might wonder why.

Why did God send an angel to Philip, rather than simply speak to him through the Spirit or the Word? On the desert road, why did God speak to him through the Holy Spirit, rather than through the angel again? Why didn't God send an angel directly to the Ethiopian or speak to him through the Spirit? If the man was already reading a Christ-centered portion of the Bible, why was Philip needed at all? Clearly God was speaking at many levels, not just one, for a reason.

Perhaps for such an unexpected command, Philip needed a startling encounter, not just a subtle, internal voice, so God sent an angel. Once the situation was clear, the Spirit could prompt Philip quietly. In either case, Scripture alone wasn't specific enough to send Philip to Gaza, and he needed detailed revelation about what to do there. Yet the Scripture was the perfect vehicle of revelation for the Ethiopian—although he still needed a human messenger to explain it to him. Clearly God's voice is varied, and the appropriate messenger in one moment might not be the appropriate messenger in another. Philip tuned in at all levels, and the Good News was carried to the continent of Africa.

> *Lord, forgive me for the ways I've limited my hearing to one or two expressions of Your voice. Speak from all angles. I'm broadening my reception to hear You everywhere.*

[Samson's] father and mother didn't realize the LORD was at work in this,

creating an opportunity to work against the Philistines,

who ruled over Israel at that time.

JUDGES 14:4

We've heard it said again and again: "God will never lead you in any way that contradicts what He has revealed in His Word." So it's a real conundrum for us when we encounter places in Scripture where God leads someone in ways that seem contrary to revelation He had already given. We see Samson defying God's orders not to marry the women of the land (Deuteronomy 7:3; Joshua 23:12-13), yet when his parents protest, Scripture tells us they didn't know God was in it. We see in Proverbs some extremely strong prohibitions about going near a prostitute, yet God leads Hosea to marry one (Hosea 1:2). And though the revelation of law hadn't been given yet, we know God in His very nature loathes child sacrifice and says so quite often. Yet He commands Abraham to take his child up on a mountain and sacrifice him—not to an idol but to God Himself. In the moment, we would have argued emphatically with all these people that they were *not* hearing God's voice. Yet they were.

God does not contradict Himself, but He also has specific guidance that may not be uniform for everyone. He doesn't defy His own nature, but we sometimes define His nature too narrowly and reduce it to rules He Himself has given. Does that mean anything goes? Of course not. But God will never call us into a relationship with principles alone. We can't just read His Word, decipher it with our minds, and say that we've heard Him. We are in a relationship with Him, and we must hear His voice as a living, dynamic reality. That stretches us, and even frustrates us at times, but it leads to a heart connection that goes well beyond words on a page. It brings us face-to-face with God.

Father, I want that—to be face-to-face with You, really hearing Your voice and not just reasoning on my own. Please lead me in Your ways.

DAY 81

Your light will shine out from the darkness,

and the darkness around you will be as bright as noon.

ISAIAH 58:10

From the Heart of God

"Do you know why I created you? Do you understand your purpose? You've gotten glimpses of it. Your confessions have captured parts of it. You are designed to glorify Me, and that involves serving and loving Me well. My Son affirmed the greatest commandments as loving Me with everything in you and loving others as yourself. These are all true, but My Word never says they are comprehensive. It only points to greater realities. You haven't seen the full picture. Your words can describe My desires for you, but they can't capture them completely. You have only begun to understand.

"I made you in My image so you could relate to Me at the most intimate levels—*and* so you could embody My nature and shine with My glory. My Son's prayer for you to share My glory gave Me great pleasure. That's My desire. I want you to be smeared with My presence—that's what 'anointing' is about—and saturated in My radiance. I once insisted that I don't share My glory with others, but I was speaking of false gods and prideful human beings. I do share My glory with My children. I want them, all of you, to emanate the brightness, the brilliance, the display of who I am.

"If My voice ever sounds demanding, this is why. It isn't because I want to hold high standards over your head; I want you to rise higher and fulfill this glorious purpose. My goal isn't to modify your behavior—animal trainers can do that. My goal is to infuse the fullness of My nature into you and let you shine. You have only begun to imagine where you're headed."

> *Oh, Lord—I can't even imagine. Your purposes for me seem so much higher than I will ever be able to attain. Only You can accomplish this, but I am willing. Let me shine brightly with Your glory.*

*[Daniel said,] "There is a God in heaven who reveals secrets."... The king
said to Daniel, "Truly, your God is the greatest of gods, the Lord over kings,
a revealer of mysteries, for you have been able to reveal this secret."*

DANIEL 2:28, 47

*K*ing Nebuchadnezzar was in a crisis because of a dream, and
Daniel's life—along with the lives of quite a few other sages—
was on the line. But Daniel knew that his God was greater
than the pressure of the situation, greater than the mystery of
the king's dream, and greater than the destiny of nations. The
question wasn't whether God knew the secret; the question was
whether He would share it with Daniel. Daniel and his friends
boldly asked God to reveal it, and God answered.

We often seek God's will on our own behalf, asking for direction and guidance for our personal lives. And while God certainly
enjoys guiding and directing us, He often has a much bigger picture in mind. He is looking for people who will listen to Him for
the solutions to society's problems. Just as He cared about revealing His will to a pagan king in Babylon, He cares about revealing
His will to governments, justice systems, school systems, medical
researchers, technological engineers, social scientists, artists and

entertainers, media outlets, agricultural planners, and more. When human need cries out for God's response, He doesn't withhold it out of some sense of judgment. He takes the opportunity to show His glory. He answers the hunger of human hearts and accepts invitations into human crises.

The problem is that there are few people like Daniel who are bold enough to believe that God might want to benefit "secular" society—or even a pagan one. But God did just that in Babylon, and it brought glory to His name and benefited His people. He will do so again—if His Daniels will appeal to the revealer of mysteries for His secrets.

Lord, You are the revealer of mysteries, and You want Your people to be blessed. Show me Your secrets. Give me Your solutions to the problems around me. Bring glory to Your name by demonstrating Your goodness to those who do not yet know You.

[The Lord said,] "Ask me and I will tell you remarkable secrets

you do not know about things to come."

JEREMIAH 33:3

*A*sk me." That's the only prerequisite God gave Jeremiah for hearing His voice. Granted, Jeremiah had been chosen for a specific purpose at a particular time in history to deliver vital messages for His people, but Jesus essentially gave hearing ears to all His people when He filled us with His Spirit. The prophets were exceptions in the Old Testament; in the New Testament era, they are examples. God pours out His Spirit on all who believe, and we all receive some level of prophetic potential (Acts 2:17-18).

"I will tell you remarkable secrets you do not know." This is the voice of a God who is eager to share His heart. He isn't withholding His mysteries. He is looking for people He can trust with them. He seeks sensitive spirits, faithful messengers, hungry souls who will pursue Him as their heart's desire. When He finds them, He unveils depths of truth we have never seen. He gives insights and inspiration that draw us closer into His heartbeat than we ever imagined possible. And He leads us into world-changing encounters with the people and culture and institutions around us. His secrets are meant to make waves in our world.

"About things to come." We long for glimpses into the future. Sometimes God gives them to us. He usually doesn't spell out the path in front of us, but He guides our steps, informs us of His greater purposes, plants desires and vision and direction within us, and prepares us for the destiny He has set before us. When we ask and draw close, He whispers the future to us.

God is excited about the future. He isn't dreading it. In Jeremiah's case, the future held correction for God's people, but it was also filled with hope. Ours is too. God longs to share His secrets with us—if we ask.

Lord, I'm asking. Whisper Your secrets to me. Prepare me for what You have planned. Draw me close to Your heart and let me hear the deep longings within it.

One day as these men were worshiping the Lord and fasting,

the Holy Spirit said, "Dedicate Barnabas and Saul for the special

work to which I have called them."

ACTS 13:2

*M*en from the church at Antioch were worshiping—some translations say "ministering to the Lord"—and they heard directly from the Holy Spirit. We don't know what that sounded like, or whether it began in the spirit of one man or in several simultaneously. We only know that this group collectively sensed a leading that they could attribute definitively to the Holy Spirit, and that it resulted in the beginning of missionary journeys to far reaches of the empire that would dramatically influence world history.

What exactly did these men hear? We know what the Spirit said, but did He speak in an audible voice? Did He influence hearts with the deep "knowing" that can't be clearly explained by those who have experienced it? Whatever the case, His words were specific and undisputed. The men knew they had heard from God.

Perhaps the bigger issue is not *how* they heard, but *what they were doing* when they heard. They were worshiping and fasting, ministering to the Lord, focused on His desires and purposes rather than their own. They weren't asking for guidance or seeking His will. They hadn't come with an agenda of what they wanted to accomplish in the world. As far as we can tell, they had nothing on their to-do list other than caring for God's heart. And that created the right environment for them to hear world-changing instructions.

One of the keys to hearing God's voice is to take a break from seeking it sometimes. It's more important to Him for us to know and love Him than it is for us to get information from Him. But when we make the relationship the priority, the instructions come. Those who seek His heart will discover what's truly on it.

Holy Spirit, I want to hear Your voice just as the men in Antioch did. But more than that, I want to express my love through worship. You are always my highest priority.

You are not controlled by your sinful nature. You are controlled by the Spirit

if you have the Spirit of God living in you.

ROMANS 8:9

I'm a sinner saved by grace." That's the declaration of nearly every Christian who understands the nature of salvation and embraces humility. And it's true; we've all come out of a sinful condition and been saved purely by grace through faith in Jesus. But it's possible to focus so much on our fallen background that we forget the glory of our current condition. Yes, we were sinners; and yes, we still sin sometimes. But that isn't God's final statement about us, and neither should it be ours. We are raised up and seated with Jesus in heaven (Ephesians 2:6) and filled, directed, and empowered by His Spirit. That's who we are.

We will never be confident in hearing God's voice unless we know this. If we focus on the fact of our sinful condition, we will always assume that our inward thoughts and impulses are of sinful origin, not prompted by the Spirit of God. We will never trust that we are being inspired and empowered by the Spirit—that it's God working in us for His pleasure (Philippians 2:13). Recognizing His voice requires recognizing the desires and thoughts He puts inside us. In order to believe He is inspiring us, we must believe that He, not our sinful nature, is the dominant force in our hearts.

Never acknowledge the depths from which you came without also acknowledging the heights to which God is taking you. To emphasize the former above the latter is to underestimate and even dishonor God's power and promises. He did not save us at such great cost for us to remain broken sinners. He only showed us that side of ourselves so we would come into His Kingdom and experience His power and life.

Spirit of God, I don't trust myself, but I trust that You are working in me in power and speaking to me and through me according to Your will. Some of my thoughts may be sinful, but many others are directly from You. Help me to trust the Holy Spirit inside me.

The letter kills, but the Spirit gives life.

2 CORINTHIANS 3:6, NIV

*N*o one has to tell a lion to roar. It just does. Why? Because that's its nature. When we strain to obey God's voice and find it difficult, we are demonstrating something about our relationship to His Word: It's *not* our nature. Clearly that's often true; we are in a lifelong process of transformation. But this is not ideal. Our goal is to grow out of that condition so that hearing from God is really a matter of being *in* Him. We want to "roar"—or serve or talk or follow His guidance—not just because He tells us to, but because it's our nature.

The letter can't accomplish that, but the Spirit can. Sadly, however, many Christians aren't continually being filled and directed by the Spirit. Most of us tend to revert to living in our own strength. We hear God's Word and set about to do it—on our own. We forget the God-given process. We are to reject our own strengths and abilities, rest in His Spirit, rely on His strength and abilities, become transformed—not by doing things, but by intimacy with Him—and then live "naturally" according to the new nature that God is working within us.

That's a deep and weighty process, but it isn't a difficult one. The yoke of Jesus is easy, and His burden is light. He lives within us so we don't have to carry the weight of life ourselves. His Spirit gives us the life we need in order to really live.

That's the difference between religion and relationship—the contrasts we so often point out but rarely experience fully and consistently. We fall back on religion far too easily. But if we can repeatedly and single-mindedly focus on God—if we can develop a Godward gaze and depend on His life within us—our inner nature will be powerfully transformed. And we will experience the Spirit who gives life.

Holy Spirit, plant Your words in me like seeds that spring to life. Let my inner nature flourish. Let Your deepest thoughts become my deepest thoughts. Live strong within me and let me rest in Your efforts.

Because we are his children, God has sent the Spirit of his Son

into our hearts, prompting us to call out, "Abba, Father."

GALATIANS 4:6

The Spirit of God puts a child's cry within us. We call out, "*Abba*," an intimately familiar term for "father"—like *Daddy*—in order to talk to our heavenly Father. We are not slaves, as Romans 8:15 assures us, but adopted and favored children in the divine family. We can assume familiarity with God. We can speak to Him on intimate terms. We can come boldly before His throne without cowering before His majesty.

If God's Spirit prompts us to speak to God in familiar, intimate language, it follows that He would speak to us in very familiar terms as well. God calls us with terms of endearment, appeals to the secrets of our hearts, and invites us to sit in His lap and experience His affection. How could He not? If He puts the cry for *Abba* within us, He will never rebuke the intimacy that follows. He allows us to speak personally to Him, and He speaks personally to us with tenderness and warmth. However closely He relates to Jesus, He relates to the Spirit of Jesus within us.

Don't let people formalize your relationship with God by

warning you about becoming "too familiar" or "too intimate." They will clothe such warnings with an appeal for "awe" and "respect"—appropriate attitudes, to be sure, but not when they undermine our childlike relationship with our heavenly Father. God, who knows how to open our hearts with just the right words, will often make His words deeply personal. They might sound frivolous to someone else, but they certainly don't to us because we know what they mean. He is speaking to a deep place in our hearts, like a father's play talk can carry enormous weight with a child. In the divine family, that's always appropriate.

Abba, my Father, You know that I respect You and bow before You. But I also need to feel Your arms around me and hear Your personal words. Speak warmly, playfully, affectionately. I need my Abba's love.

This is what the LORD, the God of Israel, says: I have heard your prayer about

King Sennacherib of Assyria. And the LORD has spoken . . . against him.

2 KINGS 19:20-21

The Assyrians had surrounded Jerusalem and were about to take over the city, enslaving its citizens, and probably killing King Hezekiah and his family. Judah's army was no match for the invaders. Defeat seemed imminent, and the Assyrian king, Sennacherib, was not reluctant to taunt, intimidate, and remind everyone of his invincibility. Hezekiah could surrender, saving the city by potentially sacrificing his own and his family's lives and submitting Judah to slavery, or he could pray and ask God to deliver His people, hoping against all hope that God would answer and avert a massacre.

Hezekiah prayed, spreading out his need before the Lord, and God heard. Isaiah prophesied Sennacherib's demise. The king would have to leave to face another enemy, and before he would be able to return and carry out his threats, he would be killed. The prophecy was fulfilled, and Assyria's army was wiped out during the night by the angel of the Lord. Sennacherib was later murdered by his own sons. Judah was saved.

Hezekiah's dilemma was resolved by the voice of God through Isaiah. Before deliverance came, deliverance was spoken. God did not leave the king in a desperate situation without any direction. He didn't prevent the desperate situation in the first place, but He did guide Hezekiah through it. Another of Judah's kings, many of whom were ungodly, might have made a catastrophic decision in that moment. But Hezekiah, stuck between choices A and B, was given a choice C—to expect miraculous deliverance. God's voice allowed him to cooperate with the divinely ordained outcome.

That's why we need to pray, wait, and listen. God has solutions, but we can experience them only if we know to cooperate with them. And we can know them only if we present our need, listen closely, and believe.

I have impossible situations too, Lord. Please speak into them. Turn back the threats, reverse the momentum, and open doors of opportunity. Let me see the miracles that come from Your mouth.

As the Scriptures say, "The facts of every case must be established by

the testimony of two or three witnesses."

2 CORINTHIANS 13:1

I was struggling, wondering whether God had changed His mind about the calling He had given me. Numbers 23:19 rose up from my memory—it declares that because God is not a man, He neither lies nor has any need to change His mind. I printed the verse and taped it above my desk, perhaps trying to convince myself that it must be true in my situation. Every day— no, numerous times a day—I stared at the verse and repeated it emphatically to myself and to God, in case He needed any reminding about it. As the verse implies, He has never made a promise and not carried it through.

Yet I had to keep reminding myself that God is faithful even when visible circumstances seem to indicate otherwise. A few days later, when I was struggling again, I asked some friends to pray and see if God was saying anything to them for me. They offered some encouraging words, and then one said, "I feel as if God wants you to know that He is not a man that He should lie, nor a son of man that He should change His mind." I was floored. Not surprised, just blown away by the confirmation. God spoke directly to my heart through a friend who knew absolutely nothing about the struggle within my heart.

God is not reluctant to confirm His words to us, nor is He put off by our asking. A multitude of requests may indicate a lack of faith, but a sincere appeal for confirmation does not. His Word requires that accusations be confirmed by two or three witnesses; the same principle can apply to our hearing and our insecurities about it. Has He really spoken? Ask Him. He'll say it again.

Lord, thank You for Your patience, not only to speak to dull ears like mine but to repeat Yourself when I'm not sure about what You said. I'm so grateful that You aren't focused on my imperfect hearing; You're focused on helping me understand.

DAY 90

[Jesus said,] "If you remain in me and my words remain in you,

you may ask for anything you want, and it will be granted!"

JOHN 15:7

From the Heart of God

"'Remain in Me and My words remain in you.' You struggle to understand this, but it isn't complicated. I graft My life into yours and yours into Mine; we become one. And I plant My words in you for them to grow up and bear fruit. This is why you are able to relate to Me and pray in complete faith.

"Maybe it will help if you understand what this does *not* mean. When I give you an instruction, I want you to consume it, not weigh it as an option. When I give you a promise, I want you to cling to it regardless of what you see or what anyone else says about it. When I give you encouragement, I expect you not to dismiss it as 'fluff' or underestimate its power but to be nourished by it as life-giving truth. To have My words 'abiding' or 'remaining' in you means not only to nod your head in agreement but to let them shape your identity. I speak My Father's spiritual DNA into

182

your spirit with My voice. On that basis, I give you this promise of answered prayer.

"Hold on to My words. They are more than encouragement, instruction, and promise. They are your life. They shape you. They plant seeds in your heart that will grow up and produce a harvest. They are promises that come true only when you can hold on to them without letting go, even when wind and waves try to shake you off. I honor the holy stubbornness of those who have so thoroughly embraced My words that they could not possibly give up on them without abandoning a part of themselves. Don't just hear them. Let them become unquenchably alive within you."

> *Jesus, I have longed for the fulfillment of this promise; let the condition become my reality, my experience in every area of my life. Let me find my identity—every impulse, every breath, every heartbeat—in Your words. And may the Father answer my prayers as though they come directly from You.*

SCRIPTURE INDEX

ABOUT THE AUTHOR

*C*HRIS TIEGREEN is the author of more than fifty books and study guides, including *The One Year Experiencing God's Presence Devotional, The One Year Salt and Light Devotional.* In addition, he has been a collaborative writer on more than twenty book projects and has written hundreds of magazine and newspaper articles, ranging from cultural commentary to inspirational devotionals to features on ministry and international missions.

Chris is a seasoned photojournalist, a student of languages, a dabbler in art, an occasional pianist, a rabid-yet-reasonable college football fan, and a zealous traveler. He especially loves beaches and Third World adventures. In addition to writing and doing photography for periodicals and books, he has been a pastor, a missionary, and a university instructor on global issues. He and his family live in Atlanta.

To learn more, visit www.chris-tiegreen.com.

GROW CLOSER TO GOD THIS YEAR WITH THOUGHTFUL AND INSPIRING DEVOTIONALS FROM ACCLAIMED WRITER CHRIS TIEGREEN.

The One Year® Walk with God Devotional

The One Year® At His Feet Devotional

The One Year® Worship the King Devotional

The One Year® God with Us Devotional

The One Year® Experiencing God's Presence Devotional

The One Year® Hearing His Voice Devotional

365 Pocket Devotions

The One Year® Heaven on Earth Devotional

More available at www.tyndale.com

REDISCOVER THE HEART & POWER OF CHRIST'S EARTHLY MISSION.

Beloved devotional author Chris Tiegreen brings readers full circle with two thought-provoking devotionals that dive deeper into the life, death, and resurrection of Christ.

THE WONDER OF ADVENT DEVOTIONAL WILL RECONNECT YOU WITH WHAT HAPPENED IN BETHLEHEM LONG AGO—AND HELP YOU EXPERIENCE IT ANEW IN YOUR LIFE RIGHT NOW.

THE PROMISE OF LENT DEVOTIONAL PREPARES YOUR HEART FOR THE IMPACT OF CHRIST'S ULTIMATE SACRIFICE—AS YOU BEGIN TO SEE THE MAGNITUDE OF GOD'S REDEMPTIVE PLAN.

AVAILABLE FROM TYNDALE MOMENTUM.   CP1302